Make Your Money Count

Keys to Unlimited Growth

Tommy Lilja

TULSA, OK

Make Your Money Count
Copyright © 2016 by Tommy Lilja Ministries
P.O. Box 700238
Tulsa, OK 74170
www.tommylilja.org
info@tommylilja.org

ISBN 978-168031-128-0

Published by:
Harrison House Publishers
Tulsa, OK 74145
www.harrisonhouse.com
Cover: Jennifer Grisham

Contents

Chapter 1

Dare to think about yourself the way God thinks about you

Every morning for about a year, I proclaimed the blessings found in Deuteronomy 28 during my morning prayer time. The first few months I needed my Bible open next to me, but it didn't take too long before I knew the first part of the chapter by heart. These are God's promises to Israel, the blessings of Abraham that now belong to us in Jesus Christ:

> *Blessed shall you be in the city, and blessed shall you be in the country. Blessed shall be the fruit of your body, the produce of your ground and the increase of your herds, the increase of your cattle and the off-spring of your flocks. Blessed shall be your basket and your kneading bowl. Blessed shall you be when you come in, and blessed shall you be when you go out.*

> *The LORD will cause your enemies who rise against you to be defeated before your face; they shall come out against you one way and flee before you seven ways. The LORD will command the blessing on you in your storehouses and in all to which you set your hand, and He will bless you in the land which the LORD your God is giving you. The LORD will establish you as a holy people to Himself, just as He has sworn to you, if you keep the commandments of the LORD your God and walk in His ways. Then all peoples of the earth shall see that you are called by the name*

of the LORD, and they shall be afraid of you. And the LORD will grant you plenty of goods, in the fruit of your body, in the increase of your livestock, and in the produce of your ground, in the land of which the LORD swore to your fathers to give you. THE LORD WILL OPEN TO YOU HIS GOOD TREASURE, THE HEAVENS, TO GIVE THE RAIN TO YOUR LAND IN ITS SEASON, AND TO BLESS ALL THE WORK OF YOUR HAND. YOU SHALL LEND TO MANY NATIONS, BUT YOU SHALL NOT BORROW. And the LORD will make you the head and not the tail; you shall be above only, and not be beneath, if you heed the commandments of the LORD your God, which I command you today, and are careful to observe them. So you shall not turn aside from any of the words which I command you this day, to the right or the left, to go after other gods to serve them.

Deut. 28:3–14 (emphasis mine)

But it would take another two years before I could fully proclaim with power and conviction what God promises us in verse 12: *"The LORD will open to you His good treasure, the heavens, to give the rain to your land in its season, and to bless all the work of your hand. You shall lend to many nations, but you shall not borrow."* Let me explain why.

One of the most common reasons we don't receive what God wants to give us is not a lack of faith. Instead, we consider ourselves unworthy of what he wants to bestow upon us. Maybe you feel, as many others do, that "I shouldn't think that I am so important," or "who am I that God would bless me with so much wealth that I would never need to borrow money again?" But the truth is that God has bigger thoughts about you than you dare to have about yourself. Sometimes God's biggest problem is convincing us of his goodness! It says that *"my God shall supply all your need according to His riches in glory by Christ Jesus."* Phil. 4:19. So he will, "according to his riches," "in glory," "supply all your need." That means that God wants to share his incomprehensible and enormous wealth with you. He wants to give you everything you need.

> So you have to dare to think the same thoughts
> about yourself that God thinks about you.
> Take God seriously, not just about
> repentance and sanctification,
> but also about his abundant goodness.

You may be thinking, "But that will make me arrogant!" No, my friend, quite the opposite! That will make you humble, because then you will realize that, in yourself, you have not done anything to deserve such love and goodness. But Jesus paid a high price to change your life, and so now you can dare, in Jesus' name, to open yourself up to the entire blessing that Jesus died for you to receive. Thank God that he supplies all your need according to his riches in glory through Christ Jesus!

Don't be so concerned with what other people think about you. Instead, dare to think and receive all of the good things that God thinks about you. After all, in the end, it is what he thinks about you, and not what other people think about you, that counts, right?

Live what you are praying for

Even though the promises of the Bible are incredible, it is important that your emotions don't cause you to speak out what you don't have faith for! It is easy to simply proclaim the words that a Biblical truth contains, without being mindful of the seriousness behind those words.

The Biblical promises aren't something you test with an attitude of "Well, if it works, it works."

If you are praying for something, you are also expected to hold on firmly to what you have prayed for. You can't pray one day that God will make you so rich that you can lend money to the nations, but the next day complain that you can't afford to give some extra money to missions. James writes that: *"But let him ask in faith, with no doubting, for he who doubts is like a wave of the sea driven and tossed by the wind. For let not that man suppose that he will receive anything from the Lord; he is a double-minded man, unstable in all his ways."* James 1:6–8. So don't rush into prayer; think first, and then pray.

> When I pray, I intend to firmly
> hold onto what I have prayed for
> until it becomes a reality.

That means that from now on, you must speak and act based on what you have prayed. It means that you stay consistent, always in agreement with yourself. You become one with your faith. You take God seriously and that is what God is — he is for real.

Steps in faith have unimaginable consequences

After two years of prayer and meditation on Deuteronomy 28, I finally had the courage and faith to pray out the remaining promise of the Lord's blessing. So with a loud voice I boldly proclaimed:

"Father, in the name of Jesus, I thank you that you can't lie, and I know that your Word is true. It is written that you will make me so rich that I won't need to borrow money and that I will even be so rich that I will be able to lend money to other nations. Thank you that these promises will now become a reality in my life."

I remember a heavy feeling of powerlessness came over me when I realized my prayer would have direct consequences on my life right away! From then on, I couldn't borrow money! Not for my own personal life or for our church building, which was in dire need of major renovations. Borrowing money for church renovations would have been the same as saying I didn't believe what God had promised me. Do you understand what I mean? If you take God seriously, you have to live out what you pray for, and the promise of God stated that *"you will not borrow money from anyone."* You can't pray you will become so wealthy that you can lend money to the nations, but then turn around and borrow money for church building renovations!

How resources that didn't exist now exist

So, what happened? Well, a few years passed, and to be honest, I didn't think too much about the prayer I had prayed. But Tommy Lilja Ministries, was experiencing explosive growth. Our ministry to help Jews home to Israel progressed more quickly than we had dared to hope. The evangelization aspect of our ministry — crusades and leadership seminars to reach the unreached with the gospel — took on proportions we could never have dreamed. And alongside all of that, our international Bible schools and humanitarian work were also growing. It was at that time, during a week of vacation in the Mediterranean, that the Holy Spirit once again shone a light on verse 13 from Deuteronomy 28.

I have a somewhat unusual way of relaxing. I go to bed early, get up at the crack of dawn, and always reserve the first hours of the morning for prayer and Bible reading. That week I prayed and meditated on the blessings in chapter 28, and one day, just as the sun was rising, a powerful anointing came over me. I felt the Holy Spirit touch my heart as I realized that what I had prayed several years before had become a reality! It was an overwhelming discovery. Huge amounts of money had been going forth from our ministry to the nations of the world. We were lending out money the way God does when he lends out money: without asking for anything in return. *"And if you lend to those from whom you hope to receive back, what credit is that to you? For even sinners lend to sinners to receive as much back. But love your enemies, do good, and lend, hoping for nothing in return; and your reward will be great."* Luke 6:34–35.

Of course, the money was not my own. I usually point out that I don't own any of it since our ministry is a collaboration that includes the work of many people. But the money was there, and it was under my stewardship within the framework of what Tommy Lilja Ministries was doing. We gave to children's villages, children's camps, disaster relief, Bible schools, leadership seminars; we employed pastors and funded church plants, helped Jews home to Israel and reached the nations with the gospel. Out of nothing, God had created resources that were now touching three continents.

On more than one occasion, we have been astonished to see resources that simply weren't available suddenly appear when they were needed. With tears in our eyes and a growing fear of God in our hearts, we have been amazed to see how the hand of God provides. He has "supplied all our need in glory" whenever we have done what he told us to do.

A little step of faith leads to a bigger step of faith

Now you might be wondering how things went with our church renovations. Quite well! The wonderful church that I have been a member of since I was baptized was built in 1964. The church members had done a good job of paying off the mortgage for the building but in 2004, forty years later, nothing had been renovated, and everything basically looked the way it had when the church was built. I remember calculating how much the necessary renovations were going to cost, and the final number was so big that if we had borrowed that kind of money, it would have taken 15 years to pay it back. Plus a loan was not an alternative. Every time that alternative was brought up, there was a voice inside of me that said, "You will not borrow from anyone." So, what did we do? We divided the renovation into stages. Each stage would cost a bit more than what we could afford, and each new stage was more expensive than the previous one. In other words, the final stage was the most expensive. It turned out to be an excellent method to have each stage of renovation be more expensive and demand a bigger step of faith than the previous stage. In the beginning, many people asked themselves how we would even get it done and whether there would be enough money. They felt that we had gotten in over our heads. But with each completed stage of renovations, the church's faith grew, and before the final stage, the negative tone had been replaced with people saying things like "We can do this; God is with us," and "The Lord is going to bless us," and "All things are possible for those who believe." The personal growth that we all experienced also illustrates an important principle for how faith grows.

Start with small things, end with the big things

Start in the small things and be honest with yourself: you only have the faith that you have! Things certainly won't get better by you pretending you have bigger faith than what you have! Besides that, Jesus teaches us that even if faith is only as big as a mustard seed, it can have a powerful effect. So do what we did when we renovated the church: take a small step of faith. When you see that it works, take a bigger step. It is more important to take a small, but successful step of faith, than a big step that fails. When you see that faith actually works, you dare to take new steps of faith. Failures, however, tend to create doubt. So always reach a bit beyond your own resources and possibilities. If you do that, you will see that in a few years, your faith and your steps of faith will grow. That's what happened in our church. Today our church is fully renovated and its financial standing is just as good as it was before the renovations were started. Not only that, but faith in what God can do has grown for many. Praise be to God!

The basic condition for financial blessing

Now you might be wondering how this is possible, and what could cause such a miraculous release of financial resources. There is a lot of teaching and advice on this topic, but there is one basic condition that has to be met.

He removed poverty from us

When Jesus identified himself with sin in the final hours of his life, he traded places with the sinner and took the consequences of sin for every single person. He himself became the very curse that had rested upon every human since Adam. There was no other way for creation to be redeemed. The curse gained its power through the disobedience of Adam, and its power could only be broken by the obedience of the second Adam. Jesus was obedient even unto death. That is why the curse and its consequences can be lifted off of every person who receives Jesus as their savior and Lord: *"[T]hat the blessing of Abraham might come upon the Gentiles in Christ Jesus, that we might receive the promise of the Spirit through faith."* Gal. 3:14.

It is not common to hear teaching on what the curse has meant for us humans. That is why it is helpful to study Deuteronomy 28 because it compares the blessing and the curses in the same chapter. We can read that when the curse exercises its effect on the area of poverty, its results are *"hunger, thirst, and nakedness, and need of everything."* Deut. 28:48.

That was why Jesus, during his final hours on the cross, took upon himself the fullness of the curse of poverty. He was hungry and thirsty, because he had not eaten or drunk anything for more than a full day. He was totally naked, which was why the disciples and followers around Jesus stood at a distance (they didn't want to embarrass him). When Jesus died, he was as poor as a human can be. He lacked everything from physical necessities to human value. Everything had been stripped from him.

Why? To remove poverty from you and me. The fall of man brought the curse upon creation and one of the consequences was poverty. But in the same way that Jesus took our punishment so that we could be forgiven, our sin so that we could be sanctified, our disease so that we could be healed, and our death so that we could have eternal life; in the same way, he also took our poverty: *"For you know the grace of our Lord Jesus Christ, that though He was rich, yet for your sakes He became poor, that you through His poverty might become rich."* 2 Cor. 8:9.

All Christians believe Jesus died so we could have eternal life. But some people doubt and even disagree that Jesus also became poor so we could have financial wealth. It makes me wonder, would it have been harder for Jesus to take upon himself the poverty of the world than our very death? Of course not! Or was Paul wrong when he wrote that Jesus became poor so that we could become rich? Absolutely not. Remember: *"He who did not spare His own Son, but delivered Him up for us all, how shall He not with Him also freely give us all things?"* Rom. 8:32.

So what is the problem? The problem is the word "rich." We tend to think about that word the way the world does, and so we attach incorrect values to it. We associate rich with multi-millionaires, selfishness, and greed. But if we replace these values with things like generosity, humanitarian work, helping the needy, fighting poverty and financing evangelistic crusades, "rich" gains the meaning that it has in the kingdom of God. As we will see in chapter two, riches in the world and riches in the kingdom of God are complete and total opposites. God wants to make you rich in the sense that he, in a glorious way, will supply all of your needs. And he won't do it so that you can become a tightwad or a selfish hoarder who only thinks of yourself!

God doesn't give because of what we do, but because of what Jesus did

When God, through Jesus, changes a person, he does it in a complete and total way. He doesn't just restore us spiritually and give us eternal life. No, he restores us body, soul and spirit. From the first day you come into Christ, God wants to change every area of your life. That is what Jesus' three words on the cross meant.

When Jesus cried out, "It is finished," that word "finished" means that which is perfect has been brought to full completion. When God redeemed man back to himself, it was a perfect work that encompassed all areas of life. He lifted off the curse and made things "perfect," so that in a "perfect" way, he could bring those who believe out of the grips of the curse and into the glory of the blessing. When God gave his only son Jesus as a sacrifice in our place, he didn't leave anything to chance. It was a "perfect" mission and when Jesus cried out "It is finished," that which was perfect was been brought to full completion, and there was nothing else that needed to be done. In every single way that sin had polluted and destroyed mankind, in every area in which the curse had exercised its power, now a "perfect" deliverance and restoration could be received in its place.

This book is about one particular area of restoration: the financial one. It has been written under the inspiration of the Holy Spirit for you who believe, so that you, in your own personal life, church, company or organization, can receive and be good stewards of this aspect of the riches that are one part of salvation: financial wealth.

Bible verses to pray and meditate on

The foundation

Christ has redeemed us from the curse of the law, having become a curse for us (for it is written, "Cursed is everyone who hangs on a tree"), that the blessing of Abraham might come upon the Gentiles in Christ Jesus, that we might receive the promise of the Spirit through faith. Gal. 3:13–14

The exchange

For you know the grace of our Lord Jesus Christ, that though He was rich, yet for your sakes He became poor, that you through His poverty might become rich. 2 Cor. 8:9

The provision

And my God shall supply all your need according to His riches in glory by Christ Jesus. Phil. 4:19

The love

He who did not spare His own Son, but delivered Him up for us all, how shall He not with Him also freely give us all things? Rom. 8:32

The promise

And the LORD will grant you plenty of goods. . . . The LORD will open to you His good treasure, the heavens . . . to bless all the work of your hand. You shall lend to many nations, but you shall not borrow. Deut. 28:18

The action

But let him ask in faith, with no doubting, for he who doubts is like a wave of the sea driven and tossed by the wind. James 1:6

Chapter 2

Does Jesus want us to be poor?

In the body of Christ, a well-meant but false teaching exalts the lack of possessions as an ideal way to live. In this teaching, riches are made out to be something ugly and unholy. It is a false doctrine that admires the aesthetic ideals of monastery life, where you leave everything behind in order to serve God behind locked doors.

But is this really what Jesus wants for your life? For you to live in poverty? To shut yourself in?

Because if that were the case, then wealth and prosperity should be something you firmly oppose.

The Christian mystics were surely loved by God, but were they obeying the Bible?

"The desert Christians were really pious," a growing number of leaders in circles of Western Christian mysticism tell us. "They found God and are role models for all of us today," they say, and challenge us to put this orthodox way of living and thinking into practice.

But I wonder how you can fulfill the Great Commission when you are shut up in a monastery or alone in the desert. The only thing you can find there is sand!

Make no mistake, Jesus' commandment to his apostles and to the church is crystal clear; our mission is to preach the gospel to all people and to the ends of the earth. Thus the poverty ideal can't be from God because it costs money to reach people groups with the gospel. And also since faith comes by hearing, it is hard to preach to unreached peoples if you have secluded yourself from the world.

So where did this poverty ideal come from? Think about it for a second. Who wants to stop the gospel from being preached? Who wants us to go in when Jesus tells us to go out, and who rejoices over poor people? It certainly isn't God! Let me explain.

In the previous chapter we saw clearly that Jesus, *"though He was rich, yet for your sakes He became poor, that you through His poverty might become rich."* 2 Cor. 8:9. So if God wants us to be poor, then why did Jesus become poor so that we could become rich?

If Jesus became poor so that we could become rich, and the ideal is for us to be poor, then God is contradicting Himself, right?

This is the same kind of false theology that claims God inflicts sickness on believers as a means of testing their faith. But if Jesus removed all of our weaknesses and diseases from us, then how could God test us using what Jesus has removed?

Would *you* use sickness as a means to influence the people you love the most?

If you had all power in heaven and on earth, would you use sickness and poverty as a means to influence and teach others a lesson — especially the ones you love the very most? Would you send a brain tumor to your best friend to teach him something, or allow your sister's child to starve to death, just to test her faith? Of course not. So what would you do? Well, you would probably make sure the ones you love are not affected by sickness or poverty. And you would teach them how to handle wealth so it would be something useful and not harmful.

If you would never do such a thing, then why would God do it? It is written that *"God is light and in Him is no darkness at all."* 1 John 1:5. He would never use evil as a means to test or influence us. In fact, it is an impossibility, since he is only light. He doesn't have any darkness to use. God is not the problem; He is the solution.

- He doesn't send the storm — He stills it!

- He doesn't make you sick — He heals you!

- He doesn't make you poor — He makes you prosper!

All evil that happens has its origin in the fall of man, and it is caused by the ruler of this world: Satan. It is Satan who has come to steal, kill and destroy, not God! This insight is quite obvious, and yet it is questioned, even among believers. Why? Because Satan has confused the world, and even some Christians, into believing that God, who is only light, sends darkness!

This crafty lie has effectively hindered people from identifying and attacking the true source of these problems: sin and Satan. Instead God gets the blame; He who is really the very solution to our problems.

Four examples that will put to death the myth of the poverty ideal

To really put to death the myth of the poverty ideal, we will now look at four examples where Jesus himself teaches on this issue. You will discover how important it is for Scripture to interpret Scripture and how Satan, with Bible verses expressed out of their context, has sown lies in the Body of Christ with the single goal of slowing down the victory march of the gospel across the earth.

Example 1: And the rest shall be given to you as well

Carina and I had been saved for a few years when I realized that most of what we had done in both our personal lives and in the ministry, including things having to do with finances, had been blessed by God. Things hadn't always been easy, but in every situation there had been an invisible hand helping us through our problems. For example, we had our house built during the major financial crisis at the start of the nineties. We moved in just when the Swedish economy had collapsed! At that time we really didn't have any revelation about "not borrowing money." Quite the opposite, when the financial crisis was at its worst, the value of our loan was greater than the value of our house. It was a hard lesson to learn. We had to keep track of every penny and carefully plan all of our purchases. My wife was an incredible accountant and she did an amazing job during those years. Even though our financial margins were minuscule after paying on the loan and other bills, we never stopped tithing and giving an offering to missions. We really believed that when you tithe and give money to the gospel, you have not only God's protection on your finances, but also a blessing that increases what you have. For many months there was no extra money at all, but God was always there in the background, giving us what we needed from the most unexpected places.

I remember one Christmas when our couch simply had to be replaced. It had been worn out for a long time, but now we could hardly sit on it and we simply did not have any money left over for a new couch. But the day before Christmas someone rang the doorbell and there in front of our house, to our surprise, was a truck from a furniture store. "I have a couch for you," the driver said, with a big smile. Someone had bought a brand new couch for us! That kind of thing happened a lot. When we couldn't see a way out, God came with an unexpected solution.

A few years ago, when I was thinking about our family's financial history, it hit me that despite our previously very tight financial situation, we had never lacked for anything. We had gone on vacation, changed cars, re-wallpapered, eventually even been able to buy new furniture, and, in one way or another, everything had always been covered. When our expenses increased, our incomes increased! Then I suddenly realized: We didn't know where the limits were for how much money we could have! Do you know what I mean? Whatever we needed, a solution was always created. Maybe now you are thinking, as I did one time, "So what are the limits for how much blessing God is prepared to give?" My answer is, I don't know. But then you might say: "So why don't you buy a Rolex watch, go to Dubai on a luxurious vacation, hire a gardener or put in a pool, just so you can figure out what the limits are?"

This question is both tempting and interesting and it leads us to the very essence of my reasoning. I will admit that during one part of my life, especially before I got saved, material riches were something I longed for. I desired luxury. I am ashamed of it today, but that doesn't make it less true. However, the day I realized that I really could get everything from God, my desire for luxury was gone. This doesn't mean, however, that I hate prosperity. Jesus has broken the curse over my life and thereby also the plague of poverty. But prosperity is not what drives me. The moment I realized that Jesus truly became poor so that I could be rich, my view of riches and possessions changed.

Both God and mammon can make you rich, but you have to choose one or the other.

So what happened? It's actually quite simple. When Jesus teaches in the Sermon on the Mount about money and wealth, he starts by giving us a choice: *"You cannot serve God and mammon."* Matt. 6:24. And then he continues by giving an example of what he means:

> *So why do you worry about clothing? Consider the lilies of the field, how they grow: they neither toil nor spin; and yet I say to you that even Solomon in all his glory was not arrayed like one of these. Now if God so clothes the grass of the field, which today is, and tomorrow is thrown into the oven, will He not much more clothe you, O you of little faith? Therefore*

do not worry, saying, "What shall we eat?" or "What shall we drink?" or "What shall we wear?" For after all these things the Gentiles seek. For your heavenly Father knows that you need all these things.

Matt. 6:28–32

Finally, he summarizes his teaching in one single sentence. *"But seek first the kingdom of God and His righteousness, and all these things shall be added to you."* v. 33.

Jesus teaches us that there are always two ways to acquire riches: by serving God or by serving mammon. However, he says, you have to choose one of them. The kingdom of God and the empire of mammon are in opposition to each other, and they can never be mixed. They are two completely different systems. Either you choose God or you choose mammon, and Jesus is very clear on this point. So let's look more closely at these two alternatives, God or mammon.

Alternative B: Serving mammon by the sweat of your brow

In the youth of creation, at the time when Adam and Eve sinned, God describes the consequence of the fall of man and the curse that it would bring upon the world: *"Cursed is the ground because of you . . . by the sweat of your brow you will eat your food."* Gen. 3:17–19 (NIV). If you choose to serve mammon, you will have to work by the sweat of your brow so that you can, in a cursed existence, earn money and build up your wealth. Any such wealth will be constantly threatened by collapse because of the curse. You won't have any protection against its negative powers. Satan is totally unreliable and you can never know how or when he will choose to harm you. So you will be in a constant state of anxiety, restlessly pursuing everything you need.

However much you have, you'll want more because you don't trust the future!

Alternative A: Serving God by faith

But there is a way out. You have to switch kingdoms and masters. By choosing God and the path of faith instead, your concerns will have a solution. Your deepest desires will be met and you can come into the rest and peace that faith provides. Why? Because everything unbelievers are pursuing, what they are scraping together by the sweat of their brow, God, your Father in heaven, already knows that you need! But not only that! You will get it from him, Jesus says, without even needing to work for it. *"Consider the lilies of the field, how they grow: they neither toil nor spin. . . . Now if God so clothes the grass of the field, which today is, and tomorrow is thrown into the oven, will He not much more clothe you?"*

Don't misunderstand me now. Jesus is not saying that you should stop working. Because *"[i]f anyone will not work, neither shall he eat."* 2 Thess. 3:10. Rather, when you work and earn money then, if you believe, the curse will not be able to exercise the same power over you as it does over those who are not in the kingdom of God! Why not? Because once you have come into the kingdom of God, you are no longer under the curse. It doesn't apply to you anymore! Your financial situation, Jesus teaches, now no longer depends on what you earn by the sweat of your brow! It depends on what he did for you on the cross!

All these things will be added to you

What Jesus is doing is opening up a new and different path to wealth: a way to earn money without the involvement of mammon and the destruction that comes along with it: *"Seek first the kingdom of God, and all these things will be added unto you."* *"All these things will be added."* I'll say it again, *"All these things will be added."* What other things? What the unbelievers are trying so hard to get! But, and this is what happened in my life, when you find God's kingdom, then *"all these things"* will take on a whole new meaning. Why? Because in God's kingdom you think in a different way than you do in the kingdom of mammon. In God's kingdom, wealth becomes a means instead of an end. Possessions become tools instead of a status symbol. So that is why I am not in the least interested in testing where the limits are. I am not striving for riches for riches' sake! I am confident in knowing that God "will supply all my need in glory" whenever a need arises.

The paradox of wealth: When you no longer desire it, then it is there in abundance!

Do you get what I am saying? As long as you are longing for what your eyes desire, what your flesh is screaming for and what your pride is boasting about, then you haven't completely found the kingdom of God. Mammon is still exercising an influence over your life. You will be in a constant rush to pursue riches and — no matter how much you own — you will never be satisfied.

But when you have found the kingdom of God
and realize that God is giving you everything you need,
even what the unbelievers are striving for,
then riches will take on a completely new value
and your perspective will change.
You become content.
Wealth is now a means instead of an end.

The worship of mammon is replaced with seeking God's will for your life, and that is what you will hunger for. As Jesus put it: *"My food is to do the will of Him who sent Me, and to finish His work."* John 4:34.

God is not a business method!

I also want to be clear on one point and really emphasize that God is not a business method! God is not a way to get rich just for the sake of riches. Too many people have become blinded by the money once they encounter the Bible's teaching on it. They look at giving as a path to riches and at tithing as a long-term business investment. I know of unsuccessful businessmen who didn't see salvation as being primarily about salvation, but rather as a new business method! They were tricked into thinking they could use the word of God to serve mammon, but they were badly mistaken.

> The riches are there, but the path to them goes through the narrow gate, and to get through it we have to forsake our love of mammon. Once we're on the other side, our view of money will be changed forever.

Example 2: Jesus never said his disciples shouldn't own anything

Another Scriptural context that has strongly contributed (perhaps more than any other) to the myth that serving Jesus means living without possessions, is the instruction Jesus gives his disciples the first time he sends them out on their own.

> *Heal the sick, cleanse the lepers, raise the dead, cast out demons. Freely you have received, freely give. Provide neither gold nor silver nor copper in your money belts, nor bag for your journey, nor two tunics, nor sandals, nor staffs; for a worker is worthy of his food.*
>
> Matt. 10:8–10

"But," you might protest, "it says right there in black and white that you shouldn't have possessions, not even an extra set of clothes." Yes, you're right, but Jesus' teaching on this subject does not end there. Just before he allows himself to be arrested, he gives some final instructions.

> *And He said to them, "When I sent you without money bag, knapsack, and sandals, DID YOU LACK ANY-*

THING?" So THEY SAID, "NOTHING." Then He said to them, "But now, HE WHO HAS A MONEY BAG, LET HIM TAKE IT, and likewise a knapsack; and he who has no sword, let him sell his garment and buy one."

Luke 22:35–36 (emphasis mine)

"So," you wonder, "how are we to know when to leave our wallet at home and when to bring it with us?" I think that the key to these at first seemingly contradictory instructions can be found in the words: *"When I sent you without money bag, knapsack, and sandals, did you lack anything?"* To which the disciples all answered, *"No, nothing."*

The author of our faith

Jesus is the author and finisher of our faith (Hebrews 12:2). Being the author of something means that he is the one who has come up with, invented, developed or initiated something. Jesus is the author of faith! To put it simply, you could say that Jesus invented faith; it was his idea! He is also the finisher of his own invention. He has, so to speak, shown that faith works, and during his time on earth he demonstrated his invention! In faith he stilled the storm, fed 5,000 people with two fish and five loaves, walked on water, healed the sick, cast out demons and raised the dead.

The Bible school of faith

When Jesus chose the twelve, he enrolled them in his Bible school, the school of faith. One of his goals was to teach the disciples to use what he himself was the author of: faith. If you read through the gospels once again you'll see that nearly every time there was something that didn't work for the disciples, Jesus spoke to them about "faith." He was constantly telling them and teaching them to "believe." We saw this same thing in the situation earlier, where Jesus was teaching about the lilies of the field and the disciples' anxiety about clothes and daily needs. *"O you of little faith,"* Jesus said, "clothes, money and food aren't a problem if you believe." It is from this perspective we should read the instructions in Chapter 10. The disciples were sent out on their first internship in Matthew 10 to be trained to believe in all areas of life, even concerning daily needs like clothes, money and food. And the disciples were overwhelmed by what faith accomplished during their field trips when they came back. Even the "evil spirits" obeyed them in Jesus' name and they "lacked nothing."

So when Jesus in John 16:31 stated that, "now you believe," it was like a graduation speech. The disciples had doubted, their faith had been weak, small, and sometimes even non-existent, but now, on their final evening with Jesus, they got it at last — they believed! So now there was no reason for them to leave their suitcase at home when they traveled. Their training period was over, and they had passed the test. Now reality awaited and the world was waiting for them to preach the gospel to the ends of the earth through faith in the name of Jesus.

Example 3: Jesus wanted to make the young rich man even richer, not take his wealth from him!

Now as He was going out on the road, one came running, knelt before Him, and asked Him, "Good Teacher, what shall I do that I may inherit eternal life?" So Jesus said to him, "Why do you call Me good? No one is good but One, that is, God. You know the commandments: 'Do not commit adultery,' 'Do not murder,' 'Do not steal,' 'Do not bear false witness,' 'Do not defraud,' 'Honor your father and your mother.'"And he answered and said to Him, "Teacher, all these things I have kept from my youth." Then Jesus, looking at him, loved him, and said to him, "One thing you lack: Go your way, sell whatever you have and give to the poor, and you will have treasure in heaven; and come, take up the cross, and follow Me." But he was sad at this word, and went away sorrowful, for he had great possessions.

Mark 10:17–22

There are many layers to this remarkable event in Jesus' life. First of all, why did the young man own so much? The answer is easy. He had kept the Word. But then Jesus tells him that he is to give all he owns to the poor, and follow him. The problem is that many people stop reading the story here and come to the conclusion that the best thing for this young man would be to not own anything at all. But the story doesn't end there. It continues, as with so many other situations in the gospels, with a discussion among Jesus and his disciples.

Then Jesus looked around and said to His disciples, "How hard it is for those who have riches to enter the

kingdom of God!" And THE DISCIPLES WERE ASTON-
ISHED AT HIS WORDS.

v. 23 (emphasis mine)

Have you ever wondered why the disciples were astonished? The answer must be that even if they were simple men, they had stable finances. Many of them ran family businesses in the fishing industry and this in a society — the Roman Empire — where 80 percent of the population was made up of slaves. To be a free man was something remarkable, and to have your own business on top of that meant that, even in their simplicity, they were more privileged than most.

> *But Jesus answered again and said to them, "Children, how hard it is for those who trust in riches to enter the kingdom of God! It is easier for a camel to go through the eye of a needle than for a rich man to enter the kingdom of God." And THEY WERE GREAT-LY ASTONISHED, saying among themselves, "Who then can be saved?"*

vv. 24–26 (emphasis mine)

Even though Jesus must have noticed that the disciples were astonished, he further emphasized what he had just said with a parable. Now the disciples were even more distressed. This meant they couldn't be saved either! Many of them were the oldest in their family business and would therefore inherit everything as the firstborn. Some of them may have even already received their inheritance.

Now Jesus had the disciples' full attention. He looked at them and said, *"With men it is impossible, but not with God; for with God all things are possible."* v. 27.

"But," you may wonder, "why is it hard for a rich person to come into the kingdom of God?" Let us once and for all proclaim that it would be a contradiction if God, who owns all gold and silver, would have a problem with wealth. So it can't be wealth itself that Jesus is talking about. No, rather it is as Paul writes to Timothy: *"Command those who are rich in this present age not to be haughty, nor to trust in uncertain riches but in the living God, who gives us richly all things to enjoy."* 1 Tim. 6:17. The danger with riches is the risk of you becoming arrogant and losing your heart to your possessions. You put your hope in something as unsure as wealth and simultaneously become a slave to mammon. Both God and mammon produce wealth in different ways, but you can't serve both. Notice Paul's conclusion, *"God gives us richly all things to enjoy."*

Then Peter began to say to Him, "See, we have left all and followed You." v. 28.

Now it is important that we don't misunderstand Peter. Once again: If Peter and the disciples no longer owned anything, then there would not have been a reason for them to be *"greatly astonished"* when Jesus said that *"it is easier for a camel to go through the eye of a needle than for a rich man to enter the kingdom of God,"* right? Remember, many of them had solid finances. They had money available to them, but the crucial difference was that whatever they owned or however much money they had control of, they had left it all to follow Jesus. In legal terms they were probably still the owners of their businesses, but they had literally given what they owned to Jesus and the gospel. They had gone from mammon to God. They no longer *"trusted in uncertain riches,"* but in Jesus and his kingdom.

It is after this discussion, which began with the young rich man throwing himself at Jesus' feet, that Jesus promises:

> *Assuredly, I say to you, there is no one who has left house or brothers or sisters or father or mother or wife or children or lands, FOR MY SAKE AND THE GOSPEL'S, WHO SHALL NOT RECEIVE A HUNDRED-FOLD now in this time — houses and brothers and sisters and mothers and children and lands, with persecutions — and in the age to come, eternal life.*

vv. 29–30 (emphasis mine)

Jesus always had a purpose with what he did and said. He used the discussion with the rich man to teach about one of the basic principles of wealth. What he said in summary was *"Peter, John, and all of you other disciples: You have certainly left everything and placed everything you own into my service and that of the gospel. But don't think that you need to live in poverty, because already here and now, in this age, you will get a hundredfold back. Whatever you have left behind, I promise you a hundredfold back."*

Of course! Jesus, who was and is the biggest advocate of the abolishment of poverty, who became poor so that we could become rich, obviously did not want his main leaders to live in poverty. After all, how could poverty demonstrate the abundance of God's riches? But what about the rich man and our question: Did Jesus want him to become poor? No, on the contrary, Jesus wanted him to become richer! If we read the entire context, the conclusion is crystal clear:

If the rich man had given what he had to Jesus and the gospel, then he could have received a hundredfold back, as well as eternal life in the coming age.

So why didn't he do it? Because even though he had kept God's commandments, he had lost his heart to his money and become a slave to mammon. Jesus wanted the best for him: to deliver him from mammon, transform his life and let him come into the true blessing, where he could be a steward of God's riches. But the rich young man chose to *"trust in the uncertainty of riches,"* which also proved to be his fall.

Example 4: It is more blessed to give than to receive, but how can you be blessed if you don't have anything to give?

In order to finally put to death the myth that God wants us to be poor, let's read Paul's words from Acts 20:35 where he clearly quotes Jesus' own words about how *"it is more blessed to give than to receive."* But how can you be blessed if you don't have anything to give? "I give love," someone might say. That is wonderful, and you should be honored for that. The cold world in which we live needs lots of love. But *"if a brother or sister is naked and destitute of daily food, and one of you says to them, "Depart in peace, be warmed and filled," but you do not give them the things which are needed for the body, what does it profit?"* James 2:15–16.

In summary, we can say that:

- Jesus promised that "all these things would be added" and he was very clear that he meant what the unbelievers strived for — material wealth.

- Jesus did not instruct the apostles or us to, as many monks in monasteries do, live without possessions. Quite the opposite, he told them and us to "bring your money bag," and why bring a money bag unless you have money in it?

- He also promised that when we "give everything for his sake and the gospel's," we will receive a hundred times more back here and now, even common and earthly things like houses, friends and possessions; everything we need.

- Jesus taught us to be careful and always distinguish between God and mammon. You can't serve both and you absolutely cannot use God to serve mammon!

- The word "rich" means one thing in the kingdom of mammon and another thing in the kingdom of God. The problems arise when Christians, who have not left mammon, talk about money in God's kingdom.

- Finally, Jesus encourages us to become happy through giving. "It is more blessed to give than to receive." But how could someone who has nothing be able to give to a world where so many are trapped by the plague of poverty? It doesn't work!

No, and that isn't Jesus' intention either, because he wants to "supply all our needs" so that we can give "what we ourselves have received as a gift."

Bible verses to pray and meditate on

Satan's purpose

"Satan has come to steal, kill, and destroy." John 10:10

The kingdom of Mammon

"Cursed is the ground because of you, through painful toil you will eat food from it... By the sweat of your brow you will eat your food." Gen. 3:17–19

The kingdom of God

"But seek first the kingdom of God and His righteousness, and all these things shall be added to you." Matt 6:33

The choice

"You cannot serve God and mammon." Matt 6:24

The reward

"Assuredly, I say to you, there is no one who has left house or brothers or sisters or father or mother or wife or children or lands, for My sake and the gospel's, who shall not receive a hundredfold now in this time — houses and brothers and sisters and mothers and children and lands, with persecutions — and in the age to come, eternal life." Mark 10:30

Chapter 3

Supernatural finances

It was just a day like any other, some years ago, when a close friend of mine, to his great surprise, found one hundred thousand dollars waiting for him outside the door of his office! This man and his wife had been living a mediocre Christian life for several years. Their company and family had been taking up all of their time. By coincidence they ended up at one of my meetings. Jesus was present, they witnessed a healing miracle and all of a sudden they experienced a wonderful renewal of the Holy Spirit. That evening their life path was turned back to God. They started getting active in their home church and their joy returned. However, they were struggling financially and not keeping up with their tithing. It was at that time the wife encouraged her husband to get better about tithing and giving offerings to missions. The husband calculated how many months back they had neglected their tithe and then gave that amount of money to their church. The very next day they found one hundred thousand dollars waiting outside the door of their office! This event was the start of a fantastic time for them. Today they are solvent and market leaders in their business in Sweden.

This story is just one of many that have come to us over the past few years. We have received so many testimonies of how people who have given to our mission projects or work in Israel have watched in amazement as their finances are blessed in a supernatural way. So what is really happening? What is it that could lead to having one hundred thousand dollars waiting outside the door? In order to arrive at the answer, I have to start from the beginning. Come along with me, because it's going to be an exciting ride!

A dualistic world with two parallel financial systems

At first glance, the world seems to simply consist of what you can see and touch. In every age of man, however, people have been able to sense an invisible dimension of reality, a spiritual realm that, even though it can't be seen, affects everything in a tangible way. The religions of the world are man's attempt to understand and tame this spiritual dimension, but they are all stumbling in the dark. When Jesus was born into our world, he was God coming in the flesh, in a physical body. And one of the many reasons for his coming was to partially explain the spiritual dimension for you. He stepped into this world from the other realm to give you guidance on how to relate to the part of the world that you can neither see nor touch. He came to give you light!

Two kingdoms

The world is basically divided into two kingdoms: God's kingdom and Satan's kingdom. They represent two alternative systems (world orders) for how the world can progress, function and be governed. One is built upon a lie and rebellion against God, while the other one is built upon the truth — the foundation upon which the world was created.

Two kinds of laws

There are also two kinds of laws that govern our existence. These are the laws of nature and the spiritual laws. The laws of nature can be proven on the basis of scientific experiments. The spiritual laws can be proven through faith and experience. But both kinds exist and provide conditions for our existence.

One example of a law of nature is the law of gravity, which shares something in common with the spiritual laws: you can't see it. But everyone knows that we have to obey the law of gravity properly, otherwise it will harm us. If you open up a window on the eleventh floor of a tall building and disregard the law of gravity by taking a step out into the open air, you will helplessly fall to the ground and die. But the laws of nature aren't just dangerous. When you know about them, you can also use them to your advantage!

It's the same way with the spiritual laws. You can't see the spiritual laws, but they are there. You don't know everything about how they work, but Jesus explained enough for you to be able to relate to them in a successful way.

The most important insight here is that the spiritual laws are superior to the laws of nature. Let me explain: God is

Spirit and in the beginning, the Spirit of God hovered over the earth. So the Spirit existed before the physical realm.

The physical realm that we can see is a consequence of what first happened in the spiritual dimension.

That is why the spiritual laws are superior to the laws of nature. The spiritual world is a prerequisite for the existence of the physical world. This truth that the spiritual is superior to the physical is clear in the life of Jesus. He demonstrated the supremacy of the spiritual over the physical when he walked on water, healed the sick, made trees wither and resurrected the dead. He acted based on a spiritual perspective, in the power of the Spirit and with unlimited spiritual power.

Two spiritual laws

The spiritual laws can also be divided into two main groups: the law of sin and death, and the law of the Spirit of life.

> *There is therefore now no condemnation to those who are in Christ Jesus, who do not walk according to the flesh, but according to the Spirit. For the law of the Spirit of life in Christ Jesus has made me free from the law of sin and death. For what the law could not do in that it was weak through the flesh, God did by sending His own Son in the likeness of sinful flesh, on account of sin: He condemned sin in the flesh, that the righteous requirement of the law might be ful-*

filled in us who do not walk according to the flesh but according to the Spirit.

Rom. 8:1–4

The law of sin and death is the condition that came into the world through the fall of man. When you put this spiritual law into practice in your life, you will always come up short. You will get what you deserve and since none of us can live a perfect life, different kinds of "death" will be what you produce in the end. This spiritual law is the one that rules in our surroundings and it seems to have a powerful attraction on people. Not even churches are free from it; too much of church life is affected by thinking based on this law of sin and death. Too many people leave church feeling weighed down instead of lifted up because we humans think in terms of cause and effect: that you get what you deserve.

It is true that you will get what you deserve,
but only in Satan's kingdom.
That is where the law of sin and death reign supreme.
But in the kingdom of God another law reigns;
the law of the Spirit of life.

When you switch over to the law of the Spirit of life, you no longer get what you deserve! Jesus took what you deserve upon himself instead of placing it upon you. He went in under the law of sin and death with the key difference that he really did live a perfect life. That means that death did not have any power over him. But when his time had come, he chose to trade places with you and with every human who ever lived. He traded his flawless life for our lives! The consequence was that God judged and punished

Jesus for our sins and transgressions instead of punishing us.

That is why the law of the Spirit of life, one of the two spiritual laws, reigns supreme over the other law, the law of sin and death. "But how can I know that for sure?" you ask. The answer is that every time someone accepts salvation, he or she goes from the law of sin and death to the law of the Spirit of life. No matter what that person seeking salvation did, the law of the Spirit of life in Jesus Christ has the power to release every person from Satan's kingdom and thus also from the law of sin and death.

How you get what Jesus deserves

So the solution to your problems is not primarily what you do but what Jesus has done for you. When you live under the law of sin and death, the fruit of your deeds is your wages. This brings fear, stress and anxiety into your life. Scared of being unemployed, afraid of not being able to pay your bills, in fear of the car breaking down, worried that interest rates will increase, anxious that something might break. The law of sin and death causes you to become insecure, selfish, stingy and greedy, because you are being ruled by fear. That is why humans always want more; they can never feel safe or satisfied. But when you come into Christ, you can rest from your deeds.

Now your life no longer depends on what you do,
but on what Jesus has done for you!
You don't get what you deserve anymore,
you get something better –
you get what Jesus deserves!

You can go from fear to faith. When you believe, then you pay your tithe, give an offering to missions, go to work with joy, trust in God and know that Jesus became poor so that you, through his poverty, would become rich. He took all of your evil, to give you all of his goodness.

Two financial systems

This dualism exists even within your finances. There are primarily two financial systems, one which is built upon the word of God, and one which is not.

It is written that:

- *You shall not lend him your money for usury, nor lend him your food at a profit.* Lev. 25:37

- *He who does not put out his money at usury, nor does he take a bribe against the innocent. He who does these things shall never be moved.* Psalm 15:5

- *After serious thought, I rebuked the nobles and rulers, and said to them, "Each of you is exacting usury from his brother." So I called a great assembly against them.* Neh. 5:7

- *Owe no one anything except to love one another, for he who loves another has fulfilled the law.* Rom. 13:8

Our economic world order is built upon usury, interest, and the loans. The national banks, stock markets and stockbrokers are all part of a global financial game, putting innocent people's lives at risk. The engine for this is usury and interest, and the root of it is love of money (1 Tim. 6:10). The economic world order that you see today would have been impossible if God's Word had been the deciding factor.

But thankfully there is an alternative. There is a way to build up fully-functional finances without credit, usury, and interest.

"Are you saying that I shouldn't borrow money?" you wonder. The Bible's answer is that you should strive to not be in debt to anyone, because then your freedom is stolen from you. If you have loans or are thinking about taking a loan, make sure that you don't borrow so much that you become a slave of the bank. Today you can see large economies, even entire countries, that can no longer make their own financial decisions. Why? They are enslaved by debt to the credit market. It is actually quite obvious, but worth emphasizing, that there is someone bigger than the bank, financial politics and interest rates. It's God. He has a plan for your finances and a strategy for how you can get out of the debt you are trapped in and build stable, growing finances.

Let's repeat

God uses spiritual laws as a basis for what he does, and the spiritual laws are superior to the natural laws. He also works based on the law of the Spirit of life, which is superior to the law of sin and death, and he has a financial system based on the spiritual laws. So now, when we look at some Biblical principles that address finances, we have to do so based on these foundational truths.

When you put these principles into practice, you influence your financial situation based on spiritual laws, which are superior to the natural laws.

This means things will start happening that you won't be able to explain. God is going to encourage you to do things that aren't rational. You are now entering the path of faith and you will call on things that don't exist as though they already existed. You are leaving usury, interest and credit behind so that you can stand on God's promises and can be sure that what God has promised, He is able to keep.

The principles of Biblical finances in action

On a chilly fall day a few years ago, an elderly friend of mine visited a lawyer who had some bad news for him; his money was gone, and now my friend owed more money than he had available to him. But the lawyer had a solution. "I see here," he said, "that you give to Operation Great Exodus, to help the Jews return home to Israel. My suggestion is that you discontinue your giving this month, so that you have more money toward paying your bills." I should mention that at this time my friend was not a part of any church, so he gave his tithe to Tommy Lilja Ministries. My old friend thought for a moment and then answered, saying, "Don't even think about it! The Jews should get to go home to Israel. I would rather have one of my other bills go unpaid." Reluctantly, the lawyer went along with his decision.

Then something strange happened. Three days after my friend paid his tithe to Tommy Lilja Ministries, the lawyer called him up. "I don't understand this," he said. "Did you ever sign up for an extra insurance plan?" "No," my friend answered. "You know I've lived my whole life as a simple worker, so I don't have any extra insurance plans!" "Then I don't understand what's happened," the lawyer said in surprise, "because we got a letter today stating that an insurance policy has been paid out in your name in the sum of $10,000!"

Even today no one can explain in a natural way how the insurance policy got signed or who paid his insurance payments. But my friend stood firm on the word of God and gave to what he believed in. He acted based on the spiritual laws that are superior to the laws of nature, and the result appeared immediately. No one knows how, but the lawyer can confirm that the money, $10,000, was paid to my friend.

The upside-down world is actually the right-side-up world

When you compare the kingdom of God with the world, the kingdom of God can sometimes seem like an upside-down world. But it's not like that at all. In fact, it's the other way around! God's kingdom is the world turned right-side-up. But we have lived in the upside-down world for so long that we believe it is God's kingdom that is upside-down, when in reality it is the one that is right-side-up.

It says in Proverbs 11:24 that *"There is one who scatters, yet increases more; and there is one who withholds more than is right, but it leads to poverty."* That seems like the upside-down world to us! When you give away what you have, then surely you must have less left. But if you save and scrimp, then you must have more left over, right? But according to the word of God it's the other way around! When you give, you get more. But if you are stingy, you become poorer. Now how do we explain this? We can't explain it fully because this truth is based on the spiritual laws in a dimension we cannot see. The spiritual dimension is always participating in what we do, whether we want it to or not, and it will make sure that the generous person gets rich and the stingy person becomes poor, whether or not we can understand it or explain it!

Another verse that can't be explained based on the laws of nature is the promise that God gives us in Philippians 4:19: *"And my God shall supply all your need according to His riches in glory by Christ Jesus."* God has promised *"in glory,"* not by force or threat, to *"supply all our need."* "But," someone might say, "God can't just give and give. Where does he get his money from?" Well, don't ask me! I don't understand it either, but I know that it is true. When we believe that God gives us everything we need, spiritual laws are set in motion and the resources we need come to us. I don't know what happens in the spiritual dimension, and I don't need to know.

The Dead Sea — so rich, and yet so dead

"Give, and it will be given to you," Jesus tells us, *"good measure, pressed down, shaken together, and running over will be put into your bosom. For with the same measure that you use, it will be measured back to you."* Luke 6:38. This is a fantastic promise that Jesus gives us. When you give, you receive. But from whom? From God! He gives back a measure to you that is *"pressed down, shaken together, and running over."*

But if you save and keep everything for yourself, what happens then? Then you risk becoming like the Dead Sea! The Dead Sea is the world's "richest" sea. It keeps everything for itself because the Dead Sea has no outlet. All of the water that flows into the Dead Sea stays in the Dead Sea. There is no sea in the world that is as rich in minerals as the Dead Sea, and yet it is dead.

When a body of water doesn't have an outlet, it dies. If a body of water doesn't get to give of what it has, it suffocates. That is the point of Jesus' teaching in the verse above. "Give and you shall receive." Open the outlet so that you get circulation in your finances. Then God can add fresh, new resources.

I have seen this put into practice. When Christians who were filled with generosity gave tithe to their church and offerings to missions, results appeared immediately. God gave back in "good measure, pressed down, shaken together, and running over." But sadly, in some cases, the more they received, the stingier they became. As time passed, they reduced their outflow even though their incomes increased. Mammon had begun to influence their minds. And then, as their outlets decreased and their outflows became choked, something started to happen to their fountains that were once so clear. Their finances began to suffocate. Instead of life in their finances there was death. The richer they became, the greedier they became, and finally there was no outlet at all. Eventually their riches caused all flow to stop in their lives and they became like the Dead Sea: they had it all, but were still dead.

She opened the floodgates

One day I received a letter from a nurse who had just finished college. She had started working part-time while also becoming a student in our correspondence Bible school. She told me that her family's finances had been crippled the past few years because they'd had more children and she had been in nursing school.

On top of that, the correspondence courses cost $100 per month. She told me that she had been doubtful as to whether she really should begin to take the classes. But both she and her husband sensed that this was something that God wanted her to do. The problem was the money — they couldn't afford it. Despite all that, this nurse started the classes and one of the first courses is on finances. That was why she was writing to me. "I can't explain this, but since I started your correspondence Bible school and since we started tithing and giving to missions, we have more money left over than before! It doesn't make sense!"

She told me of how they received unexpected gifts, got raises at work and how she had received more hours at work, even though there were others who wanted those hours and whose turn it should have been to get them.

What had happened? The nurse and her husband had opened the floodgates! They had, against all sensibility, begun to give offerings while at the same time daring to trust the inner voice and let the new nurse take correspondence Bible school classes. They operated on the spiritual level, so the upside-down world became the right-side-up world. According to the way this world looks at finances, they should have become poorer, but instead their finances grew. They gave, and in return they received good measure, pressed down, shaken together, and running over.

The example above is not uncommon. I regularly receive phone calls from people who gasp excitedly that, "It really works, Pastor Tommy!" They tell me about how they sensed the Holy Spirit telling them to give to something the Lord was doing, and that they then became employed, got a raise, or received gifts or other financial blessings. Some of them had been like the Dead Sea. They only had one inflow, but when they — in faith in Jesus — opened the floodgates, they put the heavenly realm into motion. Behind the clouds, what was prepared for them and given to them was "a good measure, pressed down, shaken together, and running over."

You have to cast your bread before you can get it back

It is written, *"Cast your bread upon the waters, for you will find it after many days."* Prov. 11:1. It will come back, but the difference is that it is God who returns it and he always gives more back than you gave out!

But you have to cast your bread first before you can get it back. There are Christians who first want to receive, and then give. It is as if you were to say to the fireplace:

*"Give me some heat first,
then I'll throw in some firewood."*

That won't work! To get warmth you first have to put in some firewood. For God to be able to send the bread back, you have to cast it first.

In summary we can say that:

- There are two kingdoms: the kingdom of God and the kingdom of Satan. *God's kingdom is superior to Satan's kingdom.*

- There are two kinds of laws: the laws of nature and the spiritual laws. *The spiritual laws are superior to the laws of nature.*

- There are two basic spiritual laws: the law of the Spirit of life and the law of sin and death. *The law of the Spirit of life is superior to the law of sin and death.*

- There are two world financial systems — one is based on the word of God, the other is not. *The financial system that is based on God's word is superior to the other one.*

This means that if you choose the kingdom of God — the spiritual laws, the law of the Spirit of life and God's financial systems — you will be superior to all the rest, since they will all be under you!

- You now obey the law of the Spirit of life.

- You don't get what you deserve, you get what Jesus deserves.

- You realize that the upside-down world is actually the right-side-up world.

- You open the floodgates and give out so that fresh spring water can flow in.

- You cast your bread as a gift because you realize that in time God will send it back, now pressed down, shaken together, and running over. You get more back than you gave out.

- You live and work based on a spiritual perspective in Christ, where you call on that which is not as though it already is.

- You have gone from death to life, even concerning your finances.

Bible verses to pray and meditate on:

Get peace, freedom and faith:

"There is therefore now no condemnation to those who are in Christ Jesus, who do not walk according to the flesh, but according to the Spirit." Rom. 8:1–2

Avoid usury and interest:

"You shall not lend him your money for usury, nor lend him your food at a profit." Lev. 25:37

Strive to be debt-free:

"Owe no one anything except to love one another, for he who loves another has fulfilled the law." Rom. 13:8

Invest for growth:

"There is one who scatters, yet increases more; and there is one who withholds more than is right, but it leads to poverty." Prov. 11:24

Give and receive more in return:

"Give, and it will be given to you: good measure, pressed down, shaken together, and running over will be put into your bosom. For with the same measure that you use, it will be measured back to you." Luke 6:38

Chapter 4

When your money and God's money become one and the same

What would you say if I were to tell you that your money and God's money could be one and the same? Actually, when Jesus describes the kingdom of God in the Gospel of Matthew, he uses a parable that we don't normally associate with finances. However, this parable does illustrate clearly how the gifts that you sow into God's kingdom become a part of the work God is doing. Your money and God's money become one and the same.

The kingdom of heaven is like what happens when a woman mixes a little yeast into three big batches of flour. Finally, all the dough rises.

Matt. 13:33 (CEV)

Just as the woman worked the yeast into the flour until all the dough could rise, the same thing happens with the financial gifts that you place into the kingdom of God. Your money is like the yeast. When you give money, it is mixed and kneaded into what God is doing on the earth. When the dough has risen and is ready to bake, you can't differentiate between your own money and God's money. To put it simply: now you could say that your money is with God and his money is with you.

Of course this is not a disadvantage; rather, it is an enormously beneficial insight that the churches, ministries and Christian organizations that never seem to lack any money have had. The secret is that they have mixed their finances into the work of God, and they have made the needs of Jesus their own needs. In doing so, the money they have access to has now become indistinguishable from God's money — they are one and the same.

When Jesus' needs become our own

One chilly fall day many years ago I was attending a seminar as a newly-appointed pastor. The main speaker was an experienced apostle and crusade evangelist from Ireland. He looked rather ordinary and was actually quite mediocre when he spoke. So when he mentioned that they had started and still supported over 1000 churches in one of India's provinces, it got my attention. He himself had organized and preached in over one hundred large crusades. I still remember to this day thinking, "That must cost a lot of money. I wonder where he gets the funds for those kinds of things?" So it was quite astonishing for me to hear him say with a smile, "I have never sent out a letter asking for money and I have never taken up an offering!" I have to admit that at that moment I couldn't take him at his word. Then he claimed that, "What I have done is to try to listen to the voice of the Holy Spirit, and then I have acted on what he has said to me." What was amazing was that they always had the money they've needed. Of course there had been some close calls at times, but each time a deadline arrived, the money was available.

What our Irish brother had realized was that when the needs of Jesus become our needs, resources will always be available when the time comes to pay the expenses. The Irish apostle had given up everything to follow Jesus, and

Jesus had supernaturally provided him with everything he needed, both personally and in the ministry. He didn't consider anything his own, but rather everything he had he made available to the kingdom of God.

This is a big step to take, especially for us Westerners. Many Christians seem to be prepared to "give up their lives," but not give up their money! It is as though they consider money to be more important than their lives! What about you? If Jesus knocked on your door right now and asked you if you could help him out with $100, what would you do? I think that you would do everything you could to find $100 to give him, just as we all would. Of course you want to help Jesus. But Jesus really is knocking on your door today and giving you the chance to be a part of what he is doing. "I am evangelizing Nepal and northern India," he says. "I am setting up Bible schools all throughout the third world so that we can reach all of these poor people with my gospel. And I am building orphanages, children's hospitals and schools for the children who are growing up in the slums. I am doing so many things. The least of my brothers and sisters, the Jews, are on their way home to my land, Israel, and I have started to pour out the Spirit of prayer and mercy so that they will be saved. I have an entire world to reach with the gospel before I can come back. But the work that I do, I do through people. Everything I do in the world is happening because there are people who, in different ways, are willingly becoming a part of the work I am doing. You can be a part of it, too!"

An abundance to give to every good work

I agree that the example above can seem naive, but that doesn't make it less true. In 2 Cor. 9:8, Paul writes to the Corinthians that: *"God is able to make all grace abound toward you, that you, always having all sufficiency in all things, may have an abundance for every good work."* You may not have always felt this way, but God's Word claims that you "always" in "all things" have enough of everything! "But," you say, "that's not true: my wallet is actually quite empty right now and it has been for a long time." Then I have a question for you: Have you put the second part of the verse into practice? Where it says that you will be able to "have an abundance for every good work"? You have to put in firewood before the fireplace can provide any warmth! You have to dare to take the step of mixing your money with Jesus' money. It doesn't matter whether your wallet is empty or bulging.

$30,000 is enough for a car, right?

I'll never forget the moving testimony I heard from a Russian pastor. He and his wife had truly given up everything to serve as pastors in a new but rapidly growing church in Moscow. All of their savings had been used up, and now they only had $750 left and they desperately needed a car. At that time the new pastor happened to be at a leaders' conference and they were just about to take up an offering for an evangelistic crusade. The pastor was reluctantly thinking about how much he could give in the offering when he suddenly heard the Holy Spirit clearly tell him: "Give all you have." "Everything?" the pastor thought, "That's $750 and we need that money for a car." Just as he was arguing with himself, the offering plate came to him. He made a quick decision, opened his wallet and gave "everything." Later that evening when he was on his way home, worrying about how to tell his wife that he had given away the last of their money, his cell phone rang. It was one of his new church members, who told him that he had sensed the Spirit of God telling him to help the pastor pay for a new car. The man had already withdrawn the money from the bank and now it was waiting in an envelope. He asked the pastor if he could come by to pick up the money. "Sure I can," the pastor answered in surprise. "May I ask how much money is in the envelope?" "Well, it's not too much considering what cars cost these days," the man said, "but I put $30,000 in the envelope, and that's enough for a car, right?"

The story above is true, but that doesn't mean that you should give away everything you have! This pastor had a lot of experience in hearing the voice of the Spirit. Nevertheless, this story is an excellent example of what this chapter has been about so far: when we see the needs of the kingdom of God as our own needs, our money will be mixed and kneaded into God's work and will become a part of God's abundance of resources.

Jesus always has a solution

All of these stories — the Irish apostle, the Russian pastor, the businessman who found $100,000 dollars waiting at his door, my old friend who received money from an insurance policy that "nobody" seemed to have signed, and even my own experiences — have something in common. In all of these examples, Jesus has provided an unforeseen solution, because Jesus always has a solution! The same goes for all areas of life.

Satan, however, never has a solution to help you with your finances. Quite the opposite; he has come to steal, kill and destroy. He is the one who blocks the outlet so that the Dead Sea can take over your life and your finances. But Jesus will show you a solution to your problems and then help you get both an outflow and a growing inflow. That solution is always based on the word and there is a word for every situation in life. Jesus is the Word and the Word is the solution. It's simple, but it is absolutely true.

A word for every situation in your life

After the death of Moses, the LORD spoke to Joshua saying:

"Moses My servant is dead. Now therefore, arise, go over this Jordan, you and all this people, to the land which I am giving to them — the children of Israel. Every place that the sole of your foot will tread upon I have given you, as I said to Moses . . . No man shall be able to stand before you all the days of your life; as I was with Moses, so I will be with you. I will not leave you nor forsake you . . . Only be strong and very courageous, THAT YOU MAY OBSERVE TO DO ACCORDING TO ALL THE LAW WHICH MOSES MY SERVANT COMMANDED YOU; do not turn from it to the right

hand or to the left, that you may prosper wherever you go. THIS BOOK OF THE LAW SHALL NOT DEPART FROM YOUR MOUTH, BUT YOU SHALL MEDITATE IN IT DAY AND NIGHT, THAT YOU MAY OBSERVE TO DO ACCORDING TO ALL THAT IS WRITTEN IN IT. For then you will make your way prosperous, and then you will have good success. Have I not commanded you? Be strong and of good courage; do not be afraid, nor be dismayed, for the LORD your God is with you wherever you go.

Joshua 1:1–9 (emphasis mine)

The promises that Joshua received were all-inclusive, and no one would be able to stand against him. God would never leave him or forsake him, every place he set his foot would belong to Israel, and he would succeed in everything and be very successful. God didn't only give him promises, however; He also opened up a strategy and a solution for success. Furthermore, he told Joshua to hold on to the teaching that Moses had given him and that was now written down in the books of Moses. He was to think about these words day and night. If he acted according to those instructions in everything he did, then he would be successful in all things.

There is always a word

God didn't promise Joshua a life without problems; rather he promised that Joshua would be able to solve any problems successfully and conquer any resistance. If Joshua kept the word of God constantly before his eyes and in his thoughts, the word would help him, both with guidance and solutions. The same goes for you and me. You don't know everything about tomorrow, but you can know that no matter what happens, God has a word for that situation. Jesus has a solution for you — he always does — and it comes from the word.

Let your prayers stand on the word

"Does this work?" Absolutely. That is what Jesus taught us. *"Whatever things you ask when you pray, believe that you receive them, and you will have them."* Mark 11:24. "But I have prayed," you say. But have you had a word from God to stand on? Because if what you are praying for is in line with the Bible, then the answer to your prayer will come sooner or later.

I'm going to share some words with you that belong to us in Christ, and I really want to encourage you to stand on these words and to meditate on them in prayer every day. See the answer to prayer in your mind's eye as though you already had it in your hand. Believe the way God does: call on what does not currently exist as though it already exists.

He has a way:
Abraham's blessing is now yours in Christ

Christ has redeemed us *"that the blessing of Abraham might come upon the Gentiles in Christ Jesus, that we might receive the promise of the Spirit through faith."* Gal. 3:14. So the blessing that Abraham received is now ours. And what is this blessing? It is all-inclusive. It covers all of the aspects of life: spirit, soul and body. I have summarized the blessings from Deut. 28:1–16 below. They are yours in Christ and it says that *"all these blessings shall come upon you and overtake you, because you obey the voice of the LORD your God."*

- Blessed shall you be in the city, and blessed shall you be in the country.

- Blessed shall be your children, and everything else you own and have.

- When your enemies attack you, the Lord will help you defeat them. They will come out against you one way and flee before you seven ways.

- The Lord will command the blessing on you in everything you own and in everything to which you set your hand.

- He will bless you in the land which he is giving you.

- The Lord will give you an abundance of all good things.

- The Lord will open to you his good treasure, the heavens, to give you everything you need when you need it.

- The Lord will make you the head and not the tail. You shall be above only, and not beneath.

So, this is you. You can receive these promises and include them in your morning prayers. If you are wondering how, I am sure there are many ways for you to do this, but let me tell you what I do:

While I am praying out the word, I see the promise as if it is already fulfilled in my mind's eye, and I pray like this: "I thank you heavenly Father that I, in the name of Jesus, am blessed in the city and in the country. Thank you my children are blessed and everything I own and have is blessed," etc. When I have prayed these promises, I also see in my mind's eye that I am successful both in my hometown and in the rest of the nation. I see in my mind's eye that my children are successful and that everything I own and have is blessed.

My prayer varies over time. However — and I really want to emphasize this — prayer should never become a ritualistic chant that gets babbled while your thoughts are elsewhere. Prayer is when you see, with emotions, images and passion, what you are praying for in your mind's eye. Everything else is a waste of time.

You may be wondering when I pray for our churches and other needs too. I pray for those things in the afternoons. I usually divide up my prayer life into two sessions. In the morning I pray mostly for things that have to do with me. Then in the afternoon I pray for things that have to do with others.

He has a way:
Wealth and riches will be in your house

Praise the LORD! Blessed is the man who fears the LORD, who delights greatly in His commandments.

. . . Wealth and riches will be in his house, and his righteousness endures forever.

Psalm 112:1, 3

Some Christian ministries that serve the kingdom of God with a huge heart never give God a chance to give them anything back. They really like to give out, but they don't think that they deserve the grace of God and thus close their hearts to the good things God wants to give them. But, as we saw earlier, God doesn't give because you are "good enough"; He gives because of the atonement in Christ. That is why you can claim the Bible verse above without a guilty conscience. Pray it and then see in your mind's eye that you already have what the Word promises: "I thank you God that wealth and riches are in my life and my house."

He has a way:
He gives you power to get wealth

Then you say in your heart, "My power and the might of my hand have gained me this wealth." And you shall remember the LORD your God, for it is He who gives you power to get wealth, that He may establish His covenant which He swore to your fathers, as it is this day.

Deut 8:17–18

This is yet another Bible verse that you can show to people who doubt that God wants to give us wealth. Would God give you power to get wealth if he actually wants to you to live like the poor? Of course he wouldn't. That is why you can pray with boldness and a clear conscience: "Thank you God, that you give me power to get wealth."

He has a way:
He does for us more than we can ask or imagine

Now to Him who is able to do exceedingly abundantly above all that we ask or think, according to the power that works in us.

Eph. 3:20

This is a wonderful Bible verse. It promises that God does "above all" we ask or imagine. When you and I pray to God for help, he does "more." This is an uplifting promise. After your morning prayers, there is another gear waiting, the one that God shifts to when he does "above all" than you've asked or imagined.

He has a way:
You are no longer a slave but a son, an heir of God

But when the fullness of the time had come, God sent forth His Son, born of a woman, born under the law, to redeem those who were under the law, that we might receive the adoption as sons. And because you are sons, God has sent forth the Spirit of His Son into your hearts, crying out, "Abba,

Father!" Therefore you are no longer a slave but a son, and if a son, then an heir of God through Christ.

Gal. 4:4–7

Awhile ago we had to replace the hot water heater in our house. The plumbers who did the work rang the doorbell and asked if they could come in. They stayed in the boiler room, but if they needed to get into the house, they had to knock and ask if they could come in again. Around this time my son came to visit. Even though he has his own apartment these days, he doesn't knock when he comes in! He just comes in as he pleases, opens the fridge, takes what he wants, sits on the couch, turns on the TV and asks if there's any food in the house. Why doesn't the plumber do the same thing? Because the plumber isn't a son in the house! He is working for us, getting paid for what he is doing. That is where his rights end! Our son, however, is an heir along with his sister. He has the right of sons. He cries "Father!" and I help him with all my heart.

It's the same way with you. You are no longer a stranger to God. You are his child. He expects you to take what is yours. He is happy when you come home and say hello. So, if you haven't prayed this way before, do it now: "Thank you God, that you are my Father and I am your son/daughter. Thank you for making me an heir. Thank you that everything you have is also mine in Christ. Thank you that you can and want to give me an abundance of

all good things. I don't throw away your grace; I accept
everything that is mine in faith."

But will God do everything that He promised in his Word?

Now you might say, "How can I know for sure that God
will do everything that he has said in his Word?" That is
a good question. There is also a good answer. It is written
that *"You have magnified Your word above all Your name."*
Psalm 138:2. God has, in a promise to Himself, committed
to doing what he said. When there are people who in faith
call on him and in Jesus' name thank him for the promises
he has made, he will also make good on those promises.
He has promised himself this, and it is impossible for God
to break a promise, betray or lie. He is light and there is
no darkness in him.

There is one who will do everything he can to separate you from the promises

Satan will do everything he can to separate you from his
promises. He has many methods and unfortunately he is
often successful. Regarding Christians, he keeps some in
total ignorance, while others know the Bible inside and
out but still don't understand anything about the kingdom
of God.

One clear example is when Israel was held captive in Egypt
for four hundred years. Even though God had promised to
give them the land of Canaan as their inheritance, they had
no idea that was the case. Why not? Satan had separated

them from God's word. Then when Moses returned to set the people free by the power of God, he came with the word! He told both the people and Pharaoh what God had promised hundreds of years ago. When Israel received the word and acted on it, their deliverance became a reality.

The oldest example of how Satan separates people from the word is when the serpent deceives Eve in paradise. What does the serpent do? He separates Eve from the word by getting her to doubt the promises. When Eve doubts, Satan has the opening he needs. After that, the people are the ones who do the rest. The strategy is the same today. Satan strives to separate you from the word and from the power of God. But in John 8:31–32 Jesus says that his word will make you free. So don't let Satan steal the word from you.

By believing, seeing the reality of the word in your mind's eye, and by proclaiming the promises in prayer, you really can set all of heaven in motion. You aren't just anybody, you are a son or daughter of the most high God and you have the right, here and now, to claim the inheritance that is already yours.

Bible verses to pray and meditate on:

Mix

"The kingdom of heaven is like what happens when a woman mixes a little yeast into three big batches of flour. Finally, all the dough rises." Matt. 13:33

Act

"And God is able to make all grace abound toward you, that you, always having all sufficiency in all things, may have an abundance for every good work." 2 Cor. 9:8

Speak out

"Praise the LORD! Blessed is the man who fears the LORD, who delights greatly in His commandments. Wealth and riches will be in his house, and his righteousness endures forever." Psalm 112:1–3

See the answer to prayer

"Whatever things you ask when you pray, believe that you receive them, and you will have them." Mark. 11:24

Chapter 5

How to open up for a financial inflow!

I frequently hold leadership training courses for executive boards. One day a CEO told me a sad story about his relative who had worked hard his entire life and became a very successful businessman. When a large corporation made a bid for his company, he didn't hesitate to take their offer. Finally, he would be able to relax and spend time with his family without the constant ringing of his cell phone. He received a large sum of money: nearly 10 million dollars. After selling his company, he carefully invested his money so that he could become even richer. He hired an experienced stockbroker and the outlook was very bright: the sectors he invested in were going through a financial boom. But then it happened. The air went out of the American real estate market unexpectedly. The financial crisis came out of nowhere, the value of his stock portfolio plummeted, and in just a few months he had lost an enormous portion of his fortune, the fruit of his life's work.

Actually, a close friend of mine experienced this same thing, but on a different level. He had started working at the age of 5 when he began joining his mother in the fields. He quit school at 13 and worked in different factories for his entire life. By the age of fifty he finally had a bit of extra money, so he invested in mutual funds. What started out as $5,000 of his own savings had multiplied over the years to become close to $20,000. Since this man, who was not an active Christian, was a close friend of mine, I advised him to sell and take his profits. The answer I got was, "But that money is going to keep making me more money."

"I don't think so," I replied gently. "You've made a good profit, be satisfied with that. Sell now, and then reinvest $4,000." However, my advice was falling on deaf ears. One month later the stock market crashed, and soon after that his entire profit was gone.

Why do I tell stories like these? Because in Jesus' Sermon on the Mount, he tells us that we should save our money in more than one place.

> *Do not lay up for yourselves treasures on earth, where moth and rust destroy and where thieves break in and steal; but lay up for yourselves treasures in heaven, where neither moth nor rust destroys and where thieves do not break in and steal. For where your treasure is, there your heart will be also.*
>
> Matt 6:19–21

In the examples above, both the businessman and the blue collar worker had placed their savings in the kind of investments where rust can destroy, moths can feast and thieves can steal. Now I'm not saying that you should take your money out of the bank and hide it under your mattress. I'm not saying that you should give away everything you own, and I'm not saying that you shouldn't invest in stocks or mutual funds. So what am I saying? I am saying that you should make sure that you also save money in your heavenly account, in the place where thieves can't break in and where rust and moths can't destroy your money!

Maybe you are saying to yourself, "Well, that verse is about storing up treasure for eternity." It's true that many people interpret the Bible verses above that way. But that really isn't what Jesus is saying! He isn't talking about good deeds, evangelization or anything else, because things like these don't rust, and moths certainly can't eat a deed done in love. No, Jesus is talking about money and savings; what rust, moths and thieves can steal and destroy. Besides, what are you going to use money and savings for in eternity? I certainly don't think we'll need bills and coins when that time comes. No, Jesus means what he says, in essence, "Save your money in heaven, where it will stay safe, no matter what happens. No one can steal it, it can't be damaged, and it can't be destroyed by fire or the passing of time. Also, those investments are protected from financial crises and economic depressions. In my heavenly kingdom, your money is safe."

Where your treasure is, there your heart will be also

Then Jesus makes an important additional comment: where your treasure is, there your heart will be also. When you save your money in your heavenly account, you are going to think about what Jesus gives you in return. When everything you own is in the bank, a large part of your heart will be right there, in the bank. Besides, at the bank, usury and interest rates are the driving force of all they do — something the Bible tells us to be careful about. That is why the Bible wants us to *"command those who are rich in this present age not to be haughty, nor to trust in uncertain riches but in the living God, who gives us richly all things to enjoy."* 1 Tim 6:17.

Having all your savings in the bank is a great uncertainty, as history has shown us time and time again. History has also shown us that people who put their money into a heavenly account, who put the kingdom of God first and who have their confidence in God, survive both financial booms and economic depressions. They live their lives based on the law of the Spirit, in an alternative social system where usury, interest and laws on eating or being eaten do not exist at all. Instead, it is God who gives us the power to acquire riches and who, in a way we can't explain, gives us an abundance even if the only thing at our disposal is two fish and five loaves of bread.

But how do you save money in God's bank account? There are many ways. Let's look more closely at four of them.

Savings method 1:
Tithing

Actually, up until this point, this entire book has been all about storing up treasure in heaven. We give to God's work in faith, whether that is to the church, Israel, missions or Christian humanitarian work. You give to what heaven is doing on earth today. You mix your finances with God's finances. You make Jesus' needs your own and you open up for an outflow of your finances so that a healthy inflow can begin to come in.

I invest our money in four different areas, and when I am out teaching other believers and churches, I encourage them to do the same thing. We give our tithe, and we also give to missions (evangelization), to Israel, and to humanitarian work (we prioritize children in need).

From 5 dollars a week to a full tithe

When we were new believers, it wasn't an obvious choice for us that we would give away any of our money at all. The word "tithe" seemed very foreign to us. The months passed, however, and as we were enjoying our lives as believers more and more, we realized that we should help out. At that time it was more about solidarity than faith in our case. After careful consideration we decided to give about $5 a week. That might not sound like much, but this was at the end of the '80s, and it was a big step for us.

Now the other side of this story is that around the same time that we started to give $5 a week, Carina's father went into retirement. They still needed him at his workplace, though, so he continued to work, and by doing so received a double salary. At that point, for no reason, he started to give us $5 a week! We took that as a sign from God and increased our weekly tithe to the church from $5 to $10. To our surprise, Carina's father started to give us $10 a week! We thought this was so amazing. Our faith grew and so we doubled our weekly gift once again. Now we were giving $20 a week, which was unbelievable to us. And Carina's father started giving us $20 also! Twenty dollars a week is eighty dollars a month, which wasn't far from a true tithe (ten percent) back in 1989. Encouraged by the support of Carina's father, we made the decision that we would really start tithing — giving ten percent of our income! I remember that it was actually quite freeing to give our money to the church. The money no longer had control over us; instead, Carina and I were serving a greater purpose — the kingdom of God.

So what happened with Carina's father, you wonder? He stopped working extra and couldn't help us out anymore. But without even being an active believer, he had helped us discover the blessing of Jesus in our finances as well.

Isn't tithing legalism?

You might wonder whether you really have to give a tithe. Isn't that legalism? It depends on why you tithe. Do you tithe in faith or because you feel forced to? The first time that tithing is mentioned in the Bible is when Abraham gave a tithe to Melchizedek, the King of Salem (Jerusalem).

And the king of Sodom went out to meet him at the Valley of Shaveh (that is, the King's Valley), after his return from the defeat of Chedorlaomer and the kings who were with him. Then Melchizedek king of Salem brought out bread and wine; he was the priest of God Most High. And he blessed him and said: "Blessed be Abram of God Most High, possessor of heaven and earth; and blessed be God Most High, who has delivered your enemies into your hand." And he gave him a tithe of all.

Gen. 14:17–20

Abraham tithed in faith, not out of obligation

Abraham lived long before the law was given to Moses and Israel at Mt. Sinai. So he cannot have given a tithe on the basis that the law required it. It says that Abraham believed and his faith was counted unto righteousness. So Abraham didn't give a tithe to obey the law, but he gave in faith. He gave to Melchizedek, who was a priest of the most high God, and in Hebrews it says that Melchizedek was a shadow of Jesus.

For this Melchizedek, king of Salem, priest of the Most High God, who met Abraham returning from the slaughter of the kings and blessed him, to whom also Abraham gave a tenth part of all, first being translated "king of righteousness," and then also king of Salem, meaning "king of peace," without father, without mother, without genealogy, having neither beginning of days nor end of life, but made like the Son of God, remains a priest continually.

Heb. 7:1–3

In Galatians, Paul says that *"you are all sons of God through faith in Christ Jesus. For as many of you as were baptized into Christ have put on Christ. There is neither Jew nor Greek, there is neither slave nor free, there is neither male nor female; for you are all one in Christ Jesus. And if you are Christ's, then you are Abraham's seed, and heirs according to the promise."* Gal 3:26–29. You are of the seed of Abraham, you are an offspring of faith and you give your tithe for the same reason that Abraham did — you give in faith to what Jesus is doing today.

Jesus on tithing

But what did Jesus say about tithing? He did receive that question once, and this is how he answered:

Woe to you, scribes and Pharisees, hypocrites! For you pay tithe of mint and anise and cummin, and have neglected the weightier matters of the law: justice and mercy and faith. These you ought to have done, without leaving the others undone.

Matt. 23:23

Notice that Jesus doesn't say that they should stop tithing; they were already very careful to do that. He says that they should do the one without neglecting the other.

The churches of Acts followed what was written in the Old Testament

Somebody might say, "But in the book of Acts they didn't tithe!" I'm not completely sure of that. What we do know is that the first church gave more than a tenth; they gave everything. They sold their homes, everything they owned and came and placed it at the feet of the apostles. They lived in a fellowship of possessions. But there is nothing to support the idea that this was the pattern that the other churches followed. So how did they get their finances to work? They gave a tithe! Remember that the first churches consisted of Jews who had come to faith in Jesus. But you may wonder how did they know that they were supposed to give a tithe? Partly because that was what the rabbis taught and what every Jew of that time practiced. Plus, Paul writes in First Corinthians that: *"Now all these things happened to them as examples, and they were written for our admonition, upon whom the ends of the ages have come."* 1 Cor. 10:11.

What we sometimes forget is that during the first four hundred years of the church, there was no New Testament! Jesus, Paul, Peter and John taught everyone based on the Old Testament. Everything that they taught on, they had to find support for in the Old Testament. So what does the Old Testament say about giving? The Old Testament says that we believers should give a tithe, but not by force, since we are no longer under the law of sin and death. Instead we give in faith to Jesus and to his body, the church.

You give because you believe.
You receive because you believe.

There is something that belongs to God

One of the Bible contexts used most frequently in teaching on tithing is from the book written by the prophet Malachi.

"Will a man rob God? Yet you have robbed Me! But you say, 'In what way have we robbed You?' In tithes and offerings. You are cursed with a curse, for you have robbed Me, even this whole nation. Bring all the tithes into the storehouse, that there may be food in My house, and try Me now in this," says the LORD of hosts, "If I will not open for you the windows of heaven and pour out for you such blessing that there will not be room enough to receive it."

Mal. 3:8–10

Some people incorrectly teach that the Bible verses above have to do with the law of Moses and that the statements in them therefore don't apply to us! But if you read through the verses carefully, you will see that Malachi is not referring to the law. He is not saying that things are going badly for the people because they broke the law of Moses on tithing. No, what Malachi is saying is that the tithe belongs to God. It isn't about a decree from the Law! The tithe is something much more: it is something that belongs to God.

What would you do if your friend's paycheck ended up in your own bank account?

When you get your paycheck each month, not all of it is yours! You have been entrusted by God with an income, but not all of that money is yours.

> Ten percent is God's money and now you are given a choice. What will you do with the tenth of the money in your pocket that doesn't belong to you?

Imagine that you were mistakenly given a double salary one month, both your own and your friend's. What would you do? Of course you would contact your friend and tell him that you have his money in your account, and then you would transfer his money into his account. You certainly wouldn't use your friend's money for your own personal expenses!

It's the same way with the tithe each month. You have received God's money in your pocket, and now you have a choice. You can keep the money (it's all about what you believe in) or you can choose to give to God what belongs to him.

"But how can I give to God what belongs to God?" you ask. That's a good question. Malachi answers that one, too. You are to give your tithe to the storehouse. The church is the body of Christ and it is the storehouse of our day. It is from the church that the seed, the word, goes forth! Another example of a storehouse is Tommy Lilja Ministries, a dynamic "farming" team in which many people, working together, are sowing the word of God in fields all over the world. Through our crusades, Bible schools, leadership seminars, children's villages and in all of the projects we are responsible for, we are sowing the word of God.

The tithe is more than a decree from the law of Moses. It is a universal principle that God has sown into creation. Of all that a person earns, a tenth belongs to him. That tenth is to be reinvested into his work on the earth.

If you don't belong to a church

Today there is a significant number of Christians who don't belong to a church. I personally encourage everyone to find a church fellowship. But until you find a church, I advise you to give your tithe to storehouses like Tommy Lilja Ministries, for example, or any other ministry joined into what Jesus is doing in the world today, since the tithe is not your money. That tenth belongs to God, and who would want to or dare to use God's money for anything other than what it is intended for?!

Savings Method 2:
Giving to missions

You might think I'm being strict here, but the tithe is not even an offering! After all, you can't give away someone else's money. It isn't until you start giving more than a tenth that you have begun giving an offering. You see, it isn't until then that you are giving from your own money. You might say, "But then there won't be anything left!" Yes, there will be! When you give to missions groups who are doing evangelistic work, you are contributing to and supporting them with a gift that the Lord is placing on your heart, and Jesus promises a fantastic return on your investment. He says that everyone who gives for his sake and the sake of the gospel will receive back one hundredfold here and now (Mark 10:29–30).

Savings Method 3:
Israel and the Jews

In 1996, Carina and I traveled with Pastor Per-Inge Storm to Israel as chaplains. I had been a pastor for three years and knew nothing about Israel. But I had the best possible teacher; our week with pastor Per-Inge was wonderful. On the third day he looked at me with that deep love that characterized him and asked, "Tommy, can you teach a Bible study on Israel later today?" I nodded, while at the same time thinking, "Well, this is going to be a short Bible study since I don't know anything that the Bible says about Israel." But when I sought the Lord that afternoon, something strange happened. When I opened my Bible it was as if it found the verses on its own. Verse after verse stood out in the text and after half an hour I didn't have just a Bible study prepared; the Holy Spirit had pointed out several verses to me that clearly show how the Gentile Christians are going to help the Jewish people home to Israel. This eventually became the start of Operation Great Exodus, which by 2016, twenty years later, had helped over 20,000 Jews home to Israel. One of the verses the Holy Spirit gave me that afternoon was from Isaiah: *"The LORD God says: 'I will soon give a signal for the nations to return your sons and your daughters to the arms of Jerusalem.'"* Is. 49:22 (CEV).

Notice that it is the Lord God who says it. The signal is Jesus. When the nations see the signal, they will help the Jewish people home to Israel. That is what we are doing today. We are leading the Jewish people to the Lord's holy mount Zion, Jerusalem.

Helping the saints in Israel

In Paul's time the Gentile Christians started to help the Jewish church in Israel, and this was something that Paul was passionate about. When he was going to motivate the churches in Greece to give to the mother church in Jerusalem, he used two entire chapters of the second letter to the Corinthians! Paul really did not want anyone in the church to miss out on realizing the importance of giving.

Paul uses the generosity of the Macedonians to provoke that of the Corinthians

Moreover, brethren, we make known to you the grace of God bestowed on the churches of Macedonia: that in a great trial of affliction the abundance of their joy and their deep poverty abounded in the riches of their liberality. For I bear witness that according to their ability, yes, and beyond their ability, they were freely willing, imploring us with much urgency that we would receive the gift and the fellowship of the ministering to the saints. And not only as we had hoped, but they first gave themselves to the Lord, and then to us by the will of God. So we urged Titus, that as he had begun, so he would also complete this grace in you as well. But as you abound in everything — in faith, in speech, in knowledge, in all diligence, and in your love for us — see that you abound in this grace also.

2 Cor. 8:1–7

It's voluntary to give, but it is also a test of love — he who loves, gives!

I speak not by commandment, but I am testing the sincerity of your love by the diligence of others. For you know the grace of our Lord Jesus Christ, that though he was rich, yet for your sakes he became poor, that you through His poverty might become rich. And in this I give advice: It is to your advantage not only to be doing what you began and were desiring to do a year ago; but now you also must complete the doing of it; that as there was a readiness to desire it, so there also may be a completion out of what you have. For if there is first a willing mind, it is accepted according to what one has, and not according to what he does not have. For I do not mean that others should be eased and you burdened; but by an equality, that now at this time your abundance may supply their lack, that their abundance also may supply your lack — that there may be equality. As it is written, "He who gathered much had nothing left over, and he who gathered little had no lack."

2 Cor. 8:8–15

We guarantee that the gift will reach its destination — the way we handle the money is transparent

But thanks be to God who puts the same earnest care for you into the heart of Titus. For he not only accepted the exhortation, but being more diligent, he went to you of his own accord. And we have sent with him the brother whose praise is in the gospel throughout all the churches,[19] and not only that, but who was also chosen by the churches to travel with us with this gift, which is administered by us to the glory of the Lord Himself and to show your ready mind, avoiding this: that anyone should blame us in this lavish gift which is administered by us — providing honorable things, not only in the sight of the Lord, but also in the sight of men. And we have sent with them our brother whom we have often proved diligent in many things, but now much more diligent, because of the great confidence which we have in you. If anyone inquires about Titus, he is my partner and fellow worker concerning you. Or if our brethren are inquired about, they are messengers of the churches, the glory of Christ. Therefore show to them, and before the churches, the proof of your love and of our boasting on your behalf.

2 Cor. 8:16–24

Don't make me ashamed of you in front of the other churches when we compare how much each person has given!

Now concerning the ministering to the saints, it is superfluous for me to write to you; for I know your willingness, about which I boast of you to the Macedonians, that Achaia was ready a year ago; and your zeal has stirred up the majority. Yet I have sent the brethren, lest our boasting of you should be in vain in this respect, that, as I said, you may be ready; lest if some Macedonians come with me and find you unprepared, we (not to mention you!) should be ashamed of this confident boasting. Therefore I thought it necessary to exhort the brethren to go to you ahead of time, and prepare your generous gift beforehand, which you had previously promised, that it may be ready as a matter of generosity and not as a grudging obligation.

2 Cor. 9:1–5

The one who gives shall receive

But this I say: He who sows sparingly will also reap sparingly, and he who sows bountifully will also reap bountifully. So let each one give as he purposes in his heart, not grudgingly or of necessity; for God loves a cheerful giver.

2 Cor. 9:6–7

God is able to give you so much that you can always afford to give a generous gift

And God is able to make all grace abound toward you, that you, always having all sufficiency in all things, may have an abundance for every good work. As it is written: He has dispersed abroad, He has given to the poor; His righteousness endures forever." Now may he who supplies seed to the sower, and bread for food, supply and multiply the seed you have sown and increase the fruits of your righteousness,

2 Cor. 9:8–10

When you give, you become rich in all things

while you are enriched in everything for all liberality, which causes thanksgiving through us to God. For the administration of this service not only supplies the needs of the saints, but also is abounding through many thanksgivings to God,

2 Cor. 9:11–12

It is a test of your obedience to the gospel of Christ

while, through the proof of this ministry, they glorify God for the obedience of your confession to the gospel of Christ, and for your liberal sharing with them and all men, and by their prayer for you, who long

for you because of the exceeding grace of God in you.
Thanks be to God for His indescribable gift!

2 Cor. 9:13–14

After two thousand years, Israel has the same needs again

After having been unrepentant for nearly two thousand years, the Jews have now begun to receive Jesus as the Messiah again. As you might remember, Paul was imprisoned when he delivered the gift to the saints in Jerusalem. Soon after that the temple was destroyed and the Jews' two-thousand-year diaspora to the four corners of the earth began. With the Diaspora also came the hardheartedness that blinded them so that they couldn't realize and believe that Jesus was and is the Messiah. But since 1948 they have been back in the land and ever since a few years into this millennium, their hardheartedness has faded away. The Spirit of mercy and prayer has been poured out and the Jews are being saved and new churches are being planted.

That is why it is our responsibility, just as it was Paul's, to help the Jews in Israel who receive Jesus as Messiah. We take over where Paul left off. That is one reason that we in Tommy Lilja Ministries are a part of the revival work that is taking place among the Jews in Israel today.

We also know that it is written: *"I will bless those who bless you, and I will curse him who curses you; and in you all the families of the earth shall be blessed."* Gen. 12:3. You can never lose when you bless Israel, because when you bless Israel, you are blessed by God Himself.

Savings Method 4:
To those who have nothing

In conclusion, let me mention the one area that is the most obvious for most people: Giving to those who have nothing. It is written that: *"He who has pity on the poor lends to the LORD, and He will pay back what he has given."* Prov. 19:17.

I am very mindful of the Bible verse above. I often meet people who are in financial trouble. Then I gladly lend to the Lord. Sometimes I sneak out after dark with an envelope of money and quietly slip the money into their mailbox with a word from the Lord. Or sometimes I open my wallet and give a gift directly.

All over the world there are orphaned children who need help. Everyone can sponsor a child or two. It's not an expense; it is lending to the Lord, and he always pays back.

Together we can help many

Not everyone can do everything and no one can help everyone, but if everyone helps someone, we will help many people together. Not everyone can give the same amount, but everyone can give something. That is why I want to encourage you in these four savings methods. Give to and invest in these four areas. Even if it is a small gift, what really counts is your faith and the attitude of your heart.

1. Tithing: God's plan for the church's finances.

2. Offering to missions: to organizations that actively evangelize.

3. Blessing Israel: help Jews home, help the growing Messianic churches in Israel.

4. Humanitarian work: for the needy, the children and the poor.

This entire chapter has been about storing up treasure in heaven and saving your money in your heavenly account. The promise God has given us is that when we give to his work on the earth in faith, we are influencing events and situations in such a way that we get more back than we ever gave. And when we have needs of our own, they will be met in an abundant way.

Bible verses to pray and meditate on:

Riches are deceiving

"Command those who are rich in this present age not to be haughty, nor to trust in uncertain riches but in the living God, who gives us richly all things to enjoy." 1.Tim. 6:17

The best possible savings method

"Do not lay up for yourselves treasures on earth, where moth and rust destroy and where thieves break in and steal; but lay up for yourselves treasures in heaven, where neither moth nor rust destroys and where thieves do not break in and steal. For where your treasure is, there your heart will be also." Matt. 6:19–21

What belongs to God

"Woe to you, scribes and Pharisees, hypocrites! For you pay tithe of mint and anise and cummin, and have neglected the weightier matters of the law: justice and mercy and faith. These you ought to have done, without leaving the others undone." Matt. 23:23

Bless Israel

"I will bless those who bless you, and I will curse him who curses you; and in you all the families of the earth shall be blessed." Gen. 12:3

Lending to the Lord

"He who has pity on the poor lends to the LORD, and He will pay back what he has given." Prov. 19:17

The gospel gives a hundredfold back

"So Jesus answered and said, "Assuredly, I say to you, there is no one who has left house or brothers or sisters or father or mother or wife or children or lands, for My sake and the gospel's, who shall not receive a hundredfold now in this time — houses and brothers and sisters and mothers and children and lands, with persecutions — and in the age to come, eternal life." Mark 10:29–30

Chapter 6

Make your money count!

A few years ago a friend of mine, an American pastor, told me a story I listened to with great compassion. He was a typical warm-hearted and hard-working servant of God who always thought of everyone else before himself. "The first ten years of ministry," he told me, "I was often both worn out and wiped out. I considered it an honor to visit small churches out in the countryside that no one else visits." He and his wife had served as pastors in many small churches in the U.S. in addition to their traveling ministry. One day, though, he felt like he just couldn't do it anymore. "I came before the Lord," he confessed, with his voice quivering, "and asked him if this was really the life he had intended for me. We never had even one extra dollar. No matter how I saved and scrimped, there wasn't enough money. My shoes were worn out, the children's clothes were too small, and the food we ate was the cheapest money could buy. My family had to trust that other church members who were better off than we were would have mercy on us." It was as though the churches' prayer to God was, "Lord, if you keep our pastor humble, we will keep him poor."

"But then one day," he said, "Jesus spoke to me. He taught me how to think, speak and act and he showed me what the Bible said, what he had promised, and he gave me the keys to living in the blessing here and now. From that day Jesus changed my life. Slowly but surely he helped me to establish a healthy and strong financial foundation for my ministry in God's kingdom. I realized that this idea that believers should live in poverty was not God's plan for his children. Instead, if I was willing and obedient, I would get to eat of the good of the land."

Who did God create the gold for?

In this chapter we will go from theory into action. My goal is to give you the keys from God's Word that will release you to live based on who you are in Jesus Christ in the financial realm. That way, filled with faith, common sense, and a focus on Jesus, you can grow into the financial overflow that God has intended for us all.

When God created the world, he also created the gold, silver, and a wonderful abundance of resources. Creation was brimming with livestock, fish, fruit and berries. Into this world God placed humans. From the beginning, there was no poverty. Poverty was something that came into the world with the fall of man, and it is a consequence of the curse that sin brought along with it.

So who did God create the abundance for then?
Well, it certainly wasn't for the Devil.

And it certainly wasn't God's idea for his people — the Jews and the church — to live in poverty while the rest of the world, those who live in darkness, partake of the wealth of the world.

When you listen to certain preachers,
you almost get the sense that God has given
the blessings of wealth to those
who don't believe in him,
but given the curse of poverty to the saints.
Nothing could be further from the truth!

Why are so many people so negative toward talking about money?

There are many reasons. One is that the step from serving God to serving mammon can be very short. Paul warned the rich many times in his letters. He warned them against starting to love their money more than God, and he warned them to not put their confidence in something as uncertain as riches.

During the past few decades a false teaching has emerged in which material and worldly success have been pointed out as a way to prove that you are strong in the Lord. That is so typical of us believers; we have a tendency to go from one ditch into the other. In this case, it has gone from a false poverty theology to a false prosperity theology. This is a double fault because the term "prosperity teaching" is misleading. God wants us to be prosperous, but worldly success should never be a motive for becoming a believer.

A life that reflects the glory of God

I am therefore aware that a book like this can be misinterpreted and that some might see this teaching as a means to self-centeredness and personal riches instead of a means to more effectively serving the kingdom of God. Let me emphasize that this is not the case.

> No one will ever be able to explain
> how the glory of God's kingdom,
> this wonderful salvation, means that
> Christians should walk through life
> as marginalized, impoverished,
> second-class citizens.

Quite the opposite, I believe our lives should reflect transformation in all aspects. It should be noticeable that you are saved: spiritually, emotionally and physically. It is written that, *"You prepare a table before me in the presence of my enemies."* So people in our surroundings should see the table that God has set before us. And what is the table they should see? They should see how God *"anoints my head with oil; my cup runs over."* Psalm 23:5.

It isn't wrong to have money, but it is wrong for money to have you

If God's word has now convinced you and you willingly say, "Okay, I believe God wants to bless me here and now. I also believe that I can be successful and rich in a healthy way. But how do I start?" That is a good question. Therefore, we are going to look at five steps to help you make your money count. In the final chapter, there is also a prayer guide that will help you to pray based on who you are; not on who you used to be.

Step 1 to making your money count: Get your thoughts straightened out and think correctly!

Depending on who you are and what background you have, it will take different amounts of time for this teaching on making your money count to have an effect on your everyday life. The curse on your life was broken the day you got saved, but it can take anywhere from a month to several years before all the pieces fall into place and you get your personal finances in order.

From drug abuse to debt to a solid life in God

A good example is a close friend of mine who was drowning in debt when he got saved. He had lived as a drug addict and criminal for many years. But the Lord transformed every aspect of his life. Of course, this took time. He had previously lived such a crazy lifestyle, bringing lots of sickness upon himself and spending every penny on debt payments because of bad financial decisions. But he really turned his life around and started from scratch. He realized that he had to change everything from the ground up. God was with him and he was healed, got a job and got married, his debt was erased, and today he has both feet on the ground. His thoughts have been straightened out according to the Scripture, and prosperity has been established in his life.

Now you might ask: Is he rich? Yes, I would have to say that he is. He has everything that he needs. He isn't striving to get millions in his bank account, but I know that when he needs something, it always works out in the most extraordinary of ways because God helps him.

There's no money press in heaven, but plenty of work on the earth

I don't know what your situation looks like, but what I am trying to say is that God doesn't sneak into the bank and erase your debt. He doesn't have a money press in heaven from which he can make money materialize in your wallet. The money is here on earth.

When you believe and obey the word of God, your actions will help you to lay the foundation for a healthy financial life. In addition, God's kingdom — the spiritual realm — will influence people and events around you in a beneficial way.

At the end of the 1990s, my wife Carina worked as a biomedical analyst at a large hospital. That spring she was scheduled to work during the entire Easter holiday, just when we were having our big conference at church. Because of all the work she does behind the scenes, we really needed her at that conference. I remember how we talked at length about what to do, since she would receive time and a half pay for working holiday hours, and we really needed that extra money. However, Carina ended up taking time off instead so that we could have a fantastic Easter conference.

Two weeks later they called from the hospital. It was a Friday afternoon and there was a lack of personnel. If Carina could come in and work she would be offered triple pay! I remember how we laughed and thanked God for helping us. This is such a typical example of how God helps us when we put his kingdom first: He opens another door.

Mostly we have to work for the money, but he gives us favor so that in the end we have an abundance of resources.

Straighten out your thinking

The reason that I began by telling about my American colleague is that he and the churches he was ministering in were thinking incorrectly and it resulted in unnecessary consequences. Many people have opinions about what the Christian life should look like, but far too many don't take the time to study the Word to see if their own understanding is really in agreement with the Scripture. When my American colleague was able to straighten out his thoughts based on what God's Word really said, the financial aspect of his life could be changed.

Like hungry baby birds who swallow everything!

We Christians are often like hungry baby birds. We eat whatever gets stuffed down our throats. But just because a pastor, priest or well-known preacher says it doesn't necessarily mean that it's right. Don't eat everything you are served. Taste it, compare it with the Scripture, and if it isn't on God's menu, spit that food out again — it's poison.

Think correctly and you will experience success in your life

Many of the psalms were written by one of the world's wisest men, King Solomon. In the first chapter of the Psalms he says:

> *Blessed is the man who walks not in the counsel of the ungodly, nor stands in the path of sinners, nor sits in the seat of the scornful; but his delight is in the law of the LORD, and in His law he meditates day and night. He shall be like a tree planted by the rivers of water, that brings forth its fruit in its season, whose leaf also shall not wither; and whatever he does shall prosper.*

Ps. 1:1–5

This is the basis for everything. Think correctly, and everything you do will succeed. So how do you learn to think correctly?

1. **Don't follow advice from people who don't believe in or want to follow the Bible as God's Word.** Here we must also unfortunately include certain groups who call themselves Christians. Ungodly advice is advice that has no support from the Bible!

2. **Don't live in sin.** This does not mean that we have to live perfect lives, because no one can do that. We are going to fail and things won't always work out for us. But if you have conscious sin in your life, you have to deal with it. Otherwise you risk that the sin will become an Achilles heel, because sooner or later sin always demands a price.

3. **Don't speak badly of people or of God.** Remind yourself not to speak negatively about other people. If you are in a situation where this is happening, change the subject or walk out of the room.

4. **Think about God's Word in all that you do.** There is a word for every situation and if you act according to God's word, what would your life look like?

   a. You will "bring forth fruit in season." That is, curcumstances will be on your side. You have "timing." You can be at the *right place* at the *wrong time,* the *wrong place* at the *right time,* or at the *wrong place* at the *wrong time.* But he who is in Christ is in the *right place at the right time.*

b. You won't "wither." Rather, year after year, your life will flourish. There is no fall or winter, just constant growth.

c. Everything you do will succeed. You will prosper at all you do.

Scripture says that these things happen to those who get their thoughts in line with the word of God and act based on what the Bible says. That's why the first step into the blessings of God is to get your thoughts straightened out!

Step 2 to making your money count: Understand where the money comes from!

Everything that exists in heaven and on earth belongs to God. God permeates everything. He has always been present and when God talks about Himself, he confirms that the entire earth is his.

For every beast of the forest is Mine, and the cattle on a thousand hills. I know all the birds of the mountains, and the wild beasts of the field are Mine. "If I were hungry, I would not tell you; for the world is Mine, and all its fullness.

Ps. 50:10–12

"The silver is mine and the gold is mine" says the LORD of hosts.

Hagg. 2:8

When you are born again and come into the kingdom of God, he wants you to take part in his great wealth. There are many ways to do that. We saw how Jesus fed 5,000 men with two fish and five loaves, or how the children of Israel ate manna from heaven for 40 years. I remember one pastor who was praying for money for food. He took out his wallet, tapped it and asked God to fill it with money. "Did that help?" you wonder. Yes, it did. This pastor is legendary among the former drug addicts he ministered to. "He was a man of God," they say, with great emotion. "He didn't just have power when he prayed, we actually saw an empty wallet fill up with bills more than once!"

Where did the money come from that filled the pastor's wallet so he could satisfy the drug addicts' stomachs with food? I have no idea. I also have no idea where the gold coin that Peter took out of the fish's mouth came from. It didn't come from heaven, because then it would have been counterfeit. And it could not have come from a bank or someone else's wallet without their knowledge, because God doesn't steal. These circumstances must be considered extraordinary.

What the Bible teaches us is that God helps and provides us with what is already his, through other people and in ways that we don't always think of.

- From loan sharks

  Whoever increases wealth by taking interest or profit from the poor amasses it for another, who will be kind to the poor. Prov. 28:8 (NIV)

- From sinners

*For God gives wisdom and knowledge and joy to a
man who is good in His sight; but to the sinner He
gives the work of gathering and collecting, that he
may give to him who is good before God. This also
is vanity and grasping for the wind.* Ecc. 2:26.

- From others

  *Give, and it will be given to you: good measure,
  pressed down, shaken together, and running over
  will be put into your bosom. For with the same
  measure that you use, it will be measured back to
  you.* Luke 6:38.

- By working:

  *"For even when we were with you, we commanded
  you this: If anyone will not work, neither shall he
  eat."* 2 Thess. 3:10. *"He who has a slack hand
  becomes poor, but the hand of the diligent makes
  rich."* Prov. 10:4. *"The soul of a lazy man desires,
  and has nothing; but the soul of the diligent shall be
  made rich."* Prov. 13:4.

As you can read from the examples above, God has
different ways and uses unusual channels to *"supply all
your need according to His riches in glory by Christ Jesus."*
Phil. 4:19.

Another way, even though it is spectacular and a challenge to our imagination, is when angels intervene.

Count on the help of angels

Not long ago we sent in an application to receive financial aid from a certain organization. I knew exactly how much money we needed, but the chairman clearly indicated that our application would be declined. "Not a chance," he said. But when I prayed that afternoon, I asked God to send "ministering angels" to that specific board meeting, with the mission of causing the sum of money we needed to be granted.

The next day, the chairman called me and told me with surprise: "I don't know what got into the board yesterday. There were other items on the agenda that had higher priority, but you received most of the budget. We've never done that before." No, you haven't, I thought to myself, but this time you had unusual guests at the board meeting. If you had only known what the item on their agenda was!

Are they not all ministering spirits sent forth to minister for those who will inherit salvation?

Heb. 1:14

Angels are at our service. We can read that evil spirits and demons can influence people's thoughts, and angels can do the same thing. Angels are spoken of very little today, but ever since the Holy Spirit pointed out to me a few years ago how involved angels are in most of the events in both the Old and the New Testament, I have learned to collaborate with and ask the angels to cause things to happen in my life and in my service for the Lord. Today angels are a part of everything I do, and they are a fantastic help to me.

"But we have the Holy Spirit, isn't that enough?" someone might protest. Absolutely, but the Holy Spirit and the angels work in different ways. The Holy Spirit is inside of me; the angels, "ministering spirits," are outside of me. The Holy Spirit lives in me; the angels don't. They are sent out to serve me! The angels move stones, open cell doors, release the winds, stop donkeys, etc. The Spirit of God doesn't do that kind of thing. He is in us, and he leads us in what we should send the angels to do.

The following is one such situation. The prophet Elijah, tired, worn out and famished, is awoken by an angel from the Lord:

> *Then as he lay and slept under a broom tree, suddenly an angel touched him, and said to him, "Arise and eat. Then he looked, and there by his head was a cake baked on coals, and a jar of water. So he ate and drank, and lay down again.*

> 1 Kings 19:5-6.

The Holy Spirit gave Elijah inner spiritual strength to fight against the priests of Baal in the might of the Lord, but the food and water came from an angel of the Lord.

Let heaven orchestrate the solution

As you can see, there are many ways for God to bless you. It is important to understand that "making your money count" does not mean trying to figure out where it will come from!

If step one was to think correctly, step two is to not think at all!

Thinking correctly about how blessings will come to you is to, initially, not think about it at all! The most common mistake is trying to figure out what God is going to do. This just limits God. The solution that you have come up with is the one you believe in, and if what you believe in is not God's way, how will things turn out then? Everything he does, he does by grace, but we receive in faith. Too many times I have prayed while also trying to figure out the solution. That just left me stuck with one single solution!

Don't be so rushed. Give heaven time to orchestrate the solution, and know that it can take time. Believe and wait. Eventually the Holy Spirit will let you know what you should do — if you should do anything at all. Everything that the earth contains belongs to the Lord; everything belongs to God, and when he gives to you from what is his, he does it in a variety of ways. It is up to you to figure out how, but also to rest in this truth. Everything belongs to God, and he wants to share it with you!

Step 3 to making your money count:
Realize who you are in Christ

Many people speak about who we should become, but the Bible speaks at least just as much about who you already are. In order to be able to receive in faith and start making your money count, realize who you already are, otherwise you can't receive! If you see yourself as a boring, mediocre loser who always ends up last in line, then of course it will be hard for you to receive God's fantastic promises. That's why it is important for you to get your thoughts in alignment with the Bible. Perhaps you once were a boring, mediocre loser who always ended up last in line, but that is not who you are anymore. Now you are different: you are successful, you shine, and you are reaching the goals that you are striving for.

When you received Jesus, you were saved from the dominion of darkness and brought into the kingdom of the Son, so that you could claim your inheritance as one of the saints.

> *[G]iving thanks to the Father who has qualified us to be partakers of the inheritance of the saints in the light. He has delivered us from the power of darkness and conveyed us into the kingdom of the Son of His love.*
>
> Col. 1:12–13

You already have these blessings from God, right here and right now. *"You are of God, little children, and have overcome them, because He who is in you is greater than he who is in the world."* 1 John 4:4. Notice that it says you have overcome them, not that you will! The victory is already yours.

> *For as many as are led by the Spirit of God, these are sons of God. For you did not receive the spirit of bondage again to fear, but you received the Spirit of adoption by whom we cry out, "Abba, Father." The Spirit Himself bears witness with our spirit that we are chil-*

dren of God, and if children, then heirs — heirs of God
and joint heirs with Christ, if indeed we suffer with
Him, that we may also be glorified together.

Rom. 8:14–17

In Christ you have gone from death to life. You are now
a believer in God's kingdom. You are an heir of God here
and now, a king and a priest under Jesus. You have taken
off the old man and clothed yourself with the new one,
who is created in likeness with God, in true holiness and
righteousness. You act now based on who you are, not
based on who you've been. Just as Jesus did, you believe
and call on things that don't exist as though they already
do. All of creation sees who you are in your inner man
and wants nothing more than to partner with you. You are
no longer a slave under the law of sin and death; the law
of the Spirit of life in Jesus Christ has set you free. You
know that your life does not depend on what you've done,
but on what Jesus has done for you. In your life, grace is
abundant and reigns, and from the depth of your Spirit
you cry "Abba, Father" and he receives you as a son or
daughter in Jesus Christ.

Close your eyes and see yourself as you really are!

It is so important that the image you see of yourself when
you close your eyes and pray is the real one. You have
to methodically cleanse away the image of the "old man"
from your thoughts and replace it with the qualities of the
"new man." The world around us does all it can, through
different kinds of media, to brainwash us with the negative

image it wants us to have of ourselves. That is why it is your responsibility to tell yourself who you really are — every single morning! Every morning you should remind your sub-conscious of the image of who you really are: the way God sees you!

Speak based on who you really are

When you start to see yourself as the person you really are, you will also be able to begin to speak differently. You believe and you do what Jesus encourages us to do; you speak faith to your problems.

> *For assuredly, I say to you, whoever says to this moun-tain, "Be removed and be cast into the sea," and does not doubt in his heart, but believes that those things he says will be done, he will have whatever he says. Therefore I say to you, whatever things you ask when you pray, believe that you receive them, and you will have them.*
>
> Mark 11:23–24.

So, you no longer speak out:

- I am hopeless; instead say, *I am developing and learning from my mistakes.*

- I am unable to afford it; instead say, *If it is God's will for me to do this, there will be enough money.*

- I am unable; instead say, *I can do all things through Christ.*

- I am worthless; instead say, *I am a new, wonderful creation in Christ.*

- I always fail; instead say, *I am successful.*

- I think I'll get sick; instead say, *I believe that I am healed.*

Your new life can now begin in earnest. Your thoughts are changed, your view of yourself is transformed, and your speech is filled with faith. You expect big things from the Lord, and the Holy Spirit will begin to whisper encouraging words in your ear. You are a believer.

Remember, the moment the devil succeeds in making you doubt who you are, you will also doubt the blessings that belong to you in Jesus Christ. But as long as you identify and believe in who you are — by habit, without reasoning — you will expect the blessing of God in your life as something natural.

Step 4 to making your money count: Hang in there!

When we pray, we put heaven into motion. We can't quite understand what is happening, but from the throne of God, events are activated and their mission is to give us what we pray for. As I've described before, there is great variety to God's ways, and it's best to not try to figure out how God is going to do it. Just rest in the fact that he is going to do it.

That is why I want you to think about the following: What happens if you change your mind? And, what happens if you change your mind several times in one day? Say that one moment you pray for money to help you buy a better car, only to realize in the next moment that you don't need a car at all and instead start to pray for money to pay for a train ticket, only to realize a few hours later that a bike would be the best alternative! That makes you, as James puts it, "a wave on the sea," a doubter. You shouldn't pray until you know what it is that you want.

Sometimes it can be hard to decide. I have problems with that too, at times. My biggest problem is when God is pointing in one direction and I am pointing in another! That's happened more than once. "What do you do then?" you wonder. Well, God is not going to change his mind, so really there isn't all that much to choose from. Unfortunately, in my experience, when the answer we get from God isn't what we want him to give us, we continue to pray. What happens then? One of two things: God is good, he stands true and in the best case we realize that and fall into line. Or, we convince ourselves that what we want must be what God really wants too, even if God's Word, people around us and prophetic words point in a different direction. "But," you protest, "you can't go against your own conviction, can you?" No, you are the one who is responsible for your life. If you aren't completely sure, then you'll just have to wait. Time will tell whether or not you were wrong, and as the years pass, experience will enable you to get better at discerning God's voice and interpreting his heavenly signals.

What I am saying is that you don't first order tomato soup and then the next minute change your mind and order pea soup, only to change again to chicken soup once the chef is nearly done with your order. That creates chaos in the kitchen. Eventually the restaurant staff will refuse to serve you.

What we agree on

Another important factor to think about is that when there are several of you praying about the same thing, you have to be in agreement about it. Jesus promises that:

> *Again I say to you that if two of you agree on earth concerning anything that they ask, it will be done for them by My Father in heaven. For where two or three are gathered together in My name, I am there in the midst of them.*

Matt. 18:19–20.

This is a fantastic promise. When we come together, Jesus is there to guarantee that we get an answer to prayer. Most people know this Bible verse and it is quoted often, but have you stopped to consider that the opposite is also true?!

What two or three disagree about and pray for, I will not do.

If he promises to do what we are in agreement about, then that must also mean that he does not do what we are in disagreement about. Why would he otherwise point out the importance of agreement in prayer? We can be in disagreement about a lot of things. Just think about times you've been at a prayer meeting. Were you in agreement with all of the intercessors about what they were praying for? Maybe someone prayed and thanked Jesus for taking our disease and prayed for those who were sick, asking for them to be healed and thanking God for their healing. Then it was the next person's turn, and he or she prayed for the same people, but with the difference that they added to their prayer: "If it is your will God, let it be." What do we have here? Two intercessors who are in disagreement! One of them believes that it has happened, while the other doesn't know if it is God's will to heal!

If your wife wants to renovate the kitchen and you want a new car, you can't pray for one or both things until you are in agreement! When others are involved, find out what you agree on and start there. Then Jesus promises that we will receive what we have prayed for.

As far as "making your money count" goes, most people share their finances together with someone else. That makes it especially important for you to be in agreement. Discuss, read the Bible, use reasoning from this book, pray and discover what both of you have faith for together. Write it down, set a date, and thank God that he, in Jesus' name, gives you what you ask for. Then proclaim what you have prayed for as though you already have it.

For example, say you pray like this:

Father, in Jesus' name we (you and your spouse) now ask you to help us pay off our debts before Christmas, that both of us would receive at least a 5% raise, that we will sleep well at night, that we would love each other in our family, that the children will do well in school, that we would be successful at work, and that besides tithing we would give to the Jews, missions and charity. Thank you Father, that you give us what we are asking for in Jesus' name.

Then say every morning and evening:

Thank you Father that our debts will be paid before Christmas, that we will receive raises, that we sleep well at night, that we love each other in this family, that the children are successful in school, that we are successful at work and that besides tithing we give to the Jews, missions and charity.

You have now prayed a prayer of agreement and now you are proclaiming what you prayed for as though you already have it. *"Whatever things you ask when you pray, believe that you receive them, and you will have them."* So now, if you believe that you have received what you have prayed for, you can't:

- Change your mind! Don't ask until you know what you want!

- Pray for it again (because that means that you haven't received it).

- Speak as though you haven't received it (if you have bought a couch, you don't keep saying that you will buy a couch).

- Disagree about what is being prayed for (because whatsoever you disagree about…).

I gave $10, can I now expect $10,000 in my account?

Well, yes! It all depends on which account you are talking about. If Jesus has promised us a hundredfold back, of course he means what he says. But he has also said that we are to store up treasure where rust, moths and thieves cannot take them from you. So it doesn't necessarily mean that they will end up in your bank account. The blessings are in safe keeping, and when you need them they are activated in heaven so that you get what is yours on earth.

"But," you might protest, "it would be easier if I had them right here, within arm's reach." Yes, I can agree with you there. But then you wouldn't need faith, right? That is what separates the chaff from the wheat. We are believers. *"For the message of the cross is foolishness to those who are perishing, but to us who are being saved it is the power of God. . . . For Jews request a sign, and Greeks seek after wisdom."* 1 Cor. 1:18, 22. Believing that you have money in heaven is foolishness for most people. But, *"the foolishness of God is wiser than men."* v. 25. So what you need to bridge the foolishness, therefore, is someone who believes. Faith is God's power unto salvation in all aspects of life, even in finances.

Finally, let me emphasize two important actions necessary to make your money count.

Step 5 to making your money count: Faith and confession

The fact that you are a believer is something that God has done for you. He has redeemed you, cleansed you with Jesus' blood, made you a new creation and placed you as an heir in his kingdom. You answered yes, but it was God who convinced you. Salvation is exclusively a work of God. The Holy Spirit in you is the proof that you belong to God. Even if you don't live an intense life as a Christian, you will still be a new creation. A lot would have to happen for that light God has lit in your life to be quenched. Jesus says there will be believers who even place their light in the darkness; they live in such a way that their new creation can't be discovered. But they still go to heaven at the end of their lives.

However, that isn't the kind of life that Jesus has saved us for. As a believer, the intention is for you to do something! You are supposed to believe. This entire book has been about how you believe. Jesus continually repeated to the disciples that they should believe; that is, do something in faith. That they would pray, speak, think and act in faith.

Now it is up to you to renew your thoughts so that they come in line with the Word of God, so that you think, dream, see, speak and act in faith.

Faith is *now*. It is a perishable item. That's why you can say that your latest confession determines the fulfillment of what you are praying for now. If, during your morning prayers, you thank God that healthy finances will always characterize your life, but the very same afternoon complain that you never have any money and that you never will, then your latest confession is the one that is in effect.

> ### Your negative emotional comments can cancel what you prayed in the morning.

Therefore, be aware of yourself. Develop a life that is consistent with what you believe in. Reflect daily on your thoughts, words and actions. If your mood lets you down, if your words get away from you or if you get discouraged, realize quickly what is happening, ask for forgiveness, and proclaim what you believe in. This is the last step, but it is so important. Don't let your words, actions or behavior cancel what you are standing in faith for. Your faith must have corresponding actions.

It takes time to change, but it is possible. In my Life Coaching discussions, I usually ask the person I am coaching if he knows how to eat an elephant. There are many different answers, but the right one is: Piece by piece! If you reflect daily on the teaching in this book, then sooner or later you will develop a life of faith, and the consequences will be that you can make your money count in all aspects of life.

Summary of the 5 steps to making your money count:

Step 1: Think correctly!

- Who did God create the abundance for?

- It's not wrong to have money, but it's wrong for money to have you.

- When you believe and obey the Word of God, your actions will help you lay the foundation for a healthy financial life. Also, the kingdom of God, the spiritual realm, will influence people and events around you in a beneficial way.

Step 2: Realize that God has a variety of ways to bless you, and let heaven orchestrate the solution

- From loan sharks: *"One who increases his possessions by usury and extortion gathers it for him who will pity the poor."* Prov. 28:8

- From sinners: *"For God gives wisdom and knowledge and joy to a man who is good in His sight; but to the sinner He gives the work of gathering and collecting, that he may give to him who is good before God. This also is vanity and grasping for the wind."* Ecc. 2:26

- From others: *"Give, and it will be given to you: good measure, pressed down, shaken together, and running over will be put into your bosom. For with the same measure that you use, it will be measured back to you."* Luke 6:38

- By working: *"For even when we were with you, we commanded you this: If anyone will not work, neither shall he eat."* 2 Thess. 3:10

- Through angels: *"Are they not all ministering spirits sent forth to minister for those who will inherit salvation?"* Heb. 1:14

Step 3: Realize who you are in Christ

- Think, speak and act based on who you are in Christ.

Step 4: Wait and hang in there

- You don't first order tomato soup and then the next minute change your mind and order pea soup, only to change again to meat soup once the chef is nearly done with your order. That creates chaos in the kitchen.

- If Jesus promises to do what we are in agreement about, then that must also mean that he doesn't do what we disagree about.

Step 5: Believe and cling to your confession

- Faith is a perishable item.

- Develop a life that is consistent with what you believe in.

- Take one small step at a time.

- Reflect daily on your life.

Chapter 7

The believer's prayer guide:
See, believe and receive

The prayer guide you are now holding in your hands is a simple description of what I do when I pray, and it's just that: a guide. The very best teacher you'll ever have is the one on the inside, the Holy Spirit. So you should look at this prayer guide as simply an aid that can help you develop a more organized prayer life.

Once you've reached that point, then you and the Holy Spirit can partner to blaze new trails and create a dynamic prayer-time based on what your life is like and the situations that you find yourself in.

But I want to emphasize that the prayer of seeing, believing, and proclaiming who you are and where you are headed is a vital and necessary part of a successful Christian life. It's not a ritual performance; it's a way for you to shut out all the distractions going on around you, to wash away all the negative images the world wants to influence you with, and to come before God, who created heaven and earth.

It is during your prayer time that you can feel that you and God are one, and can rest in faith and realize that heaven is on your side. Heaven is fighting for you and working for you. You are not alone; an entire realm that you cannot see is available to help you.

Introduction

God already lives on the inside of you. When you are in prayer, you have contact with your inner man. Sometimes it can take awhile to shut out the distractions around you, while other times you are able get in contact with the spiritual dimension on the inside of you right away. But it all starts with you making that deliberate choice, every morning before doing anything else, to enter into the spiritual dimension to meet with God. That is where you will see yourself based on who you are in Christ, and in faith you'll see the future that you want to achieve as already accomplished in the here and now.

You are a believer, and you influence, change and affect the world around you based on what you believe. Your method to do this is to believe your way to change, influence and resources. You act in the natural world based on a supernatural perspective.

See what you are praying for. *"Believe that you have received it,"* Jesus said. See in your mind's eye what it is you are praying for. All of the Bible verses in this prayer guide can be visualized. It is important that you let it take the time that it needs to take until the images grow in your mind's eye.

Don't just read the Bible verses; see them in your mind's eye while you are praying them out loud! Don't let your thoughts wander; see yourself in the Word.

Dynamic prayer or a repetitive ritual? There are two ways to use this prayer guide. It can be used as just a lifeless ritual, statements that you quote out loud every morning while your thoughts are elsewhere. Or, you can use it as a vibrant experience in the Spirit, where you close your eyes and see who you are in the word of God. Use it to see in your mind's eye that the things you are praying about and asking for are already answered. You see the change you want to accomplish in your inner man as you proclaim it. You confirm your position in Jesus and allow all of God's kingdom — the heavenly realm — to be put into action so that the purpose of God in your life will be fulfilled.

I, _____, am a believer
and I influence, change, affect and
release resources by faith!

Morning prayer time:
God, Jesus, the Holy Spirit,
personal development

1. **God created the heavens and the earth.** He is always present and his creation is aware that God is God. You are also a part of creation. All of creation wants to cooperate with you.

   Morning prayer time starts with praising God for who he is and thanking him for Jesus, who is the way by which you have come into the kingdom of God. Some psalms and Bible scriptures that you can pray in variation are:

    a. Psalm 148 (everything that God has created is told to praise him)

    b. Psalm 150, Psalm 111, Psalm 48

    c. Paul's prayers: Eph. 1;15–23, 3:14–21

    d. Jesus is the way: John 10:9–10, 14:6

    e. The Lord's Prayer

2. **Your own relationship with God in Jesus** (also lift up your family).

    a. Pray for forgiveness: 1 John 1:8–9

    b. From Romans, remind yourself of who you are in Christ: 5:1, 8, 21; 6:10, 8:1–3 (you are no longer under the law of sin and death but the law of the Spirit of life)

Remember, when you read out the Scriptures above, make them personal! Put your own name in them and when you pray, see yourself in these verses and pray as if they had already happened.

3. **Below I have put together a prayer to help you get started.** Once again: don't merely recite it; live it as you pray it!

In Christ I have gone from death to life. I am now a believer in God's kingdom. I am an heir of God here and now, a king and priest under Jesus. I have taken off the old man and been clothed in the new man, who is created in the likeness of God, in holiness and righteousness. I now act based on who I am, not on who I've been. I believe as Jesus did and call on that which doesn't exist as though it already did. All of creation sees who I am in my inner man and wants nothing more than to cooperate with me. I am no longer a slave under the law of sin and death. No, now the law of the Spirit of life has set me free in Jesus Christ. I know that my life doesn't depend on what I've done, but on what Jesus has done for me. In my life, grace overflows and reigns completely, and from the depth of my Spirit I cry Abba, Father, and He receives me as a son/daughter in Jesus Christ.

4. **God is your God and he has described who he is for you** in the names that he has. Pray these names out loud and see yourself in them as promises that have already been fulfilled. He is:

    a. **The Lord your healer.** Isaiah 53: "by his wounds you are healed." You are healthy!

    b. **The Lord your righteousness.** Your own robe was stained but you have taken that off and now you are clothed in Jesus' righteousness.

    c. **The Lord who sanctifies.** You are set apart for God and you and your house will serve the Lord.

d. **The Lord who is always present.** The Holy Spirit is in you and wants to help, guide, teach and walk with you today.

e. **The Lord your joy and peace.** See yourself smiling, peaceful, humble and encouraging.

f. **The Lord who provides.** He gives you an overflow of all good things. See wealth and prosperity in your life. For help, pray from Deuteronomy 28:3–26.

g. **The Lord your victory.** God has given you victory in Jesus. No matter what problems you face, you can see yourself as a problem solver and victorious in the end. You are successful.

h. **The Lord your Shepherd.** Psalm 23. You shall not want for anything, you are well-rested, at peace and energetic, led by the word of God, unafraid, filled with faith, anointed as a king, and you rule by faith, have an abundance of all things, expect goodness and mercy all of your days and know that you are in God forever.

i. **The Lord your Lord.** In your spirit, soul and body.

5. **Put on the armor of God.** Ephesians 6:11. See yourself putting on the truth (the word of God), righteousness (Jesus), shoes (witnessing about Jesus), the helmet (you change your thinking), the shield (faith is your method), and the sword (the Word makes the decisions).

6. **That you love one another.** See yourself interacting with other people with love, always encouraging, with a soft voice, giving hope, trying to understand, being helpful and generous, and see how Jesus in you shines forth.

There is a Bible verse for every situation we are confronted with in life. If you have problems that this prayer guide doesn't cover, look for a Word in the scriptures; a promise for your situation. Then add that Bible verse to your daily prayer time. See the answer to your prayer from day one and hang in there. The answer is on its way, even if it takes time sometimes. No matter whether it's your own life, your family, work or something else, there is always a Bible verse to show the way. Find the Bible verse, receive it, see the answer and let the kingdom of God help you.

Afternoon prayer time:
Prayer for others

1. **Worship God, who created the heavens and the earth.** Worship and praise God who is present in his creation. Quote some Bible verses that you know by heart to help you focus.

2. **Visualize that the kingdom of God is available to you** so that you can work together and that all of this is possible because God is God and all of creation is his. You are in his kingdom, which is in the world, spiritually through the Spirit, physically through you!

3. **Lift up your future goals and visions.** Write down goals and visions. Be specific and set dates. See them as fulfilled when you pray. Remember! Too many people let their thoughts wander away from prayer to try to figure out how it will all work out! Let those thoughts go. Let heaven orchestrate the path to the goal. Believe as God does: call on that which doesn't exist as though it already does.

4. **Pray for the church of God, the local and the universal church.** See huge crowds of people ready to get baptized, see filled churches and people giving their lives to Jesus. See that this is possible because Jesus has all power in heaven and on earth.

5. **See Israel and the Jewish people restored in Israel.**

6. **Lift up other prayer requests**, people who are sick, etc. But if you have prayed, don't pray again, just thank God that the answer to prayer is yours! If we pray twice for the same thing, then the first prayer must have been in disbelief, right? If we have prayed, then the answer is on its way. You could also pray for people going through difficult situations, that their faith won't be crushed before the answer to prayer has become a reality.

7. **Your prayer requests.** See them in your mind's eye, pray them, and then thank God as though they have already been answered.

Renew your mind according to who you really are!

God is good. He loves you and he has a wonderful plan for your life. The purpose of this book has been to reveal one part of that plan, your finances. My wish and prayer is that you will keep going back to the truths revealed here until they become a part of you. Use the prayer guide daily. It will help you renew your mind according to who you really are, and help you fully receive who you are in the area of finances. God wants to help you make your money count!

"Following Jesus" – with Tommy

Tommy Lilja's TV program, "Following Jesus with Tommy Lilja," is being broadcast all over the world and the message is clear: Follow Jesus! Yes, healings are wonderful, counseling brings restoration, relief work is necessary and churches are the backbone of every ministry, but it all starts and ends with following Jesus. When you focus on Jesus, the rest will follow naturally. Jesus is the preeminence of all things and that is the message Tommy preaches and teaches all over the world.

Jesus loves you and he has a wonderful plan for your life. Make Jesus the preeminence in your marriage, your ministry and your finances, and the restoration you seek will come naturally. In Tommy's TV program he invites you to join him as he follows Jesus all over the world, from nation to nation, seeing lives transformed by Jesus' power and love.

TommyLilja
ministries

Tommy Lilja Gospel Crusades

When you follow Jesus with Tommy, **Believing Faith** will be implemented in your life – and it will come naturally! This picture is from Zambia in the summer of 2016. On the first night of the crusade, this boy was completely deaf and mute. He couldn't hear anything at all. The second night, when Tommy invited him up on stage and prayed for his ears, the boy gave Tommy a thumbs up! He could hear! But he still couldn't speak. Tommy prayed again and commanded him to speak in the name of Jesus. All of a sudden he made a sound! Tommy helped him to count, and the boy counted to five with difficulty because he had never talked before! By the end of the meeting he could say Jesus and Tommy. This is what Jesus is doing in the world today: children are getting healed, and people are being delivered from demonic powers. Tommy wants you to follow Jesus – so that Jesus can do the same things through you, too!

Tommy Lilja Gospel Crusades are more than just weekend conferences. Crusades generate a momentum that gets released during Tommy's visit, but its effects reverberate over a long period of time. When Jesus becomes established in a place, he will touch everything in that city, just as he does in our lives.

One example is a city on the border of Zambia and Congo. A prophecy came forth during Tommy's "Spellbreaker" message and then a year later, two big office buildings that had been empty for years were filled with businesses and jobs were created. Also, a new school opened up in the very slum where the crusade had been held, and many prostitutes came to the Lord. One of Tommy's goals in every crusade is to explain and release **Believing Faith** so that Jesus can restore the society as a whole. Jesus is the cornerstone, and whether it's your life or an entire city, when we build upon him amazing things will happen.

Operation Great Exodus

Since 1996, Tommy Lilja Ministries has been helping Jews return to Israel. Tommy's project **Operation Great Exodus** has now helped more than 20,000 Jews back home to the Holy Land. One aspect of following Jesus with Tommy is to take responsibility for the whole mission Jesus has in the world – and Jews are a vital part of what Jesus is doing.

Our goal is the return of Jesus, but before that will happen the Jews must be back in Israel. It's there that God will pour out his Spirit of prayer and grace, the veil will be removed, and the Jews will see the one whom they have pierced, and they will mourn him as their Son. The return of Jesus is to the land, the people and the city, and it is a rescue operation. The armies of a world coalition will stand at the border of Israel, a great number of Jews will be killed, and when all hope is lost and Satan

goes in for the final kill – then the heavens will open up and the rider on the white horse will descend to lead the final battle for the people he loves so much – the Jews.

To follow Jesus with Tommy is to be an integral part of bringing God's people back to Israel, which will usher in the return of Jesus.

TommyLilja
ministries

The Honor Operation

The Honor Operation is something that moves us all to tears. Orphaned street children, victims of human trafficking and victims of incest. You can find them everywhere, but in the poorest parts of the world they are rapidly growing in number. Tommy has pastors on salary at the border between Nepal and India to expose trafficking. He has undercover operations in some of the biggest brothel districts in the world, rescuing kids from being sold for sex. The ministry funds children's homes and special clinics to help victims. The girl crying in the photo was born to a prostitute at a hotel in Asia. The hotel owner kept the baby as an investment and started to sell her at the age of 8 to up to 10 customers per day. Tommy rescued her when she was a teenager. Today she is saved, restored, baptized and has been trained as a seamstress. To follow Jesus with Tommy is to restore the honor all these children were robbed of – and it's an honor to do it! A key principle of The Honor Operation is that it's never too late to rescue someone – and the same goes for you too!

TommyLilja
ministries

Join us in following Jesus all around the world!

Following Jesus with Tommy is a global mission. The needs are everywhere and you are more important than you can imagine. Why? Because only you can be you! If you are not carrying out the unique calling that God designed just for you, then no one else will! Only you can be you, and only you can do what God has called you to do. That's why Jesus is counting on you and that is the spirit of Tommy Lilja Ministries: We are working side by side – together as one body. If one of us cries, we all cry, if one rejoices, we all rejoice – and we would love for you to join us in following Jesus.

Contact:
Tommy Lilja Ministries
P.O.Box 700238
Tulsa, OK 74170

www.tommylilja.org
info@tommylilja.org

Tommy Lilja Ministries is an exempt organization as defined in Section 501(c)(3) of the U.S. Internal Revenue Code and, accordingly, donations are tax deductible to the extent allowable by the law.

PRAYER OF SALVATION

God loves you—no matter who you are, no matter what your past. God loves you so much that He gave His one and only begotten Son for you. The Bible tells us that "...whoever believes in Him shall not perish but have eternal life" (John 3:16 NIV). Jesus laid down His life and rose again so that we could spend eternity with Him in heaven and experience His absolute best on earth. If you would like to receive Jesus into your life, say the following prayer out loud and mean it from your heart.

Heavenly Father, I come to You admitting that I am a sinner. Right now, I choose to turn away from sin, and I ask You to cleanse me of all unrighteousness. I believe that Your Son, Jesus, died on the cross to take away my sins. I also believe that He rose again from the dead so that I might be forgiven of my sins and made righteous through faith in Him. I call upon the name of Jesus Christ to be the Savior and Lord of my life. Jesus, I choose to follow You and ask that You fill me with the power of the Holy Spirit. I declare that right now I am a child of God. I am free from sin and full of the righteousness of God. I am saved in Jesus' name. Amen.

If you prayed this prayer to receive Jesus Christ as your Savior for the first time, please contact us on the Web at **www.harrisonhouse.com** to receive a free book.

Or you may write to us at
Harrison House • P.O. Box 35035 • Tulsa, Oklahoma 74153

The Harrison House Vision

Proclaiming the truth and the power

Of the Gospel of Jesus Christ

With excellence;

Challenging Christians to

Live victoriously,

Grow spiritually,

Know God intimately.

Fast. Easy. Convenient.

For the latest Harrison House product information and author news, look no further than your computer. All the details on our powerful, life-changing products are just a click away. New releases, E-mail subscriptions, testimonies, monthly specials — find it all in one place. Visit harrisonhouse.com today!

harrisonhouse